THE RESOLUTE PATH

THE RESOLUTE PATH

Ayman Kafel

The
Second Mission
Foundation

Contents

PROLOGUE

"A man is great not because he hasn't failed; a man is great because failure hasn't stopped him." —*Confucius*

I dedicate this book to all those who have served before, who have paid the ultimate sacrifice, who currently serve, and those who are raising their right hands at this very moment and becoming our great nation's future protectors. Whether you're a cop walking the beat or a service member deployed overseas, you all play a role in defending our nation from all enemies, both foreign and domestic.

As the wars in Afghanistan, Iraq, and Syria wind down and new conflicts appear on the horizon, one of the most important things that veterans of these conflicts can do is to tell their stories to the next generation. One day I was talking to my friend and fellow war veteran Charlie Faint, the owner of The Havok Journal, and learned that I've submitted nearly 100 pieces to the Journal in just about two years. I was shocked that I'd written that many. He suggested that I put those submissions, which include articles and poetry, into a book. And thus this project was born.

This is not a traditional book, in so much as it is a compilation of all my articles and poems about my military and law enforcement experiences published in The Havok Journal. It is generally organized in chronological order and presented factually to the best of my memory. I am grateful to have this opportunity to share my experiences with future generations of military service members and first responders, and I thank the Second Mission Foundation staff and The Havok Journal for making this possible.

This is not just "my" story. This book is not just about highlighting combat or discussing the various operations I have been a part of in the military and as a police officer. This book is about my journey from the beginning to the present.

This book is not about the ugly part of war, but more about what occurs to combat veterans when we come home. It's about how some veterans get lost in society until they get their second mission, until they find their new purpose. I truly hope this book will inspire others to carve their own "Resolute Path."

The cover art for this book is a stock photo from Shutterstock, used here under an Enhanced License. I chose it because it sums up my own personal journey and how I have weathered life's challenges, often with a gun at my side, as I've forged my own path through this world.

To my brothers and sisters in arms, I say to you, stay on azimuth (Stay the Course) and Charlie Mike (Continue Mission).

Editors:
Linda Seme
Elizabeth Kafel
A.J. Livermore

Cover Art:
Shutterstock

PART 1: MILITARY SERVICE

THE DRIVE

What is it that makes us go,
Makes us push for that last lap,
That last rep...

What is it that makes us go,
Makes us push past our comfort zones,
Past our need dominate

Was it something in your past?
Was it something that burrowed itself deep inside?

I've seen war as a child, I've seen
pain as a child,
I've seen the destruction men can inflict upon each other
at such a young age.
Artillery raining on a mountain side,
A soldier blown up by a grenade on the ground

Is that what created this lion inside?
Is that what gave me the drive?
Is that what gave me my will and resolve?

It's a combination of it all,
It's the will and resolve.
It's The Drive; it's the Lion inside that
continuously stalks its prey.

As a man,
I've taken all my pain, anger, rage and formed it into
an unstoppable power.
I've taken my guilt, my sad-
ness, my hate
and used it to fuel my resolve.
It's The Drive that makes us push that extra mile.
It's The Drive *that helps us save lives.*
It's The Drive to protect.
The Drive *is deep inside you.*
Dig deep and find it.

1

A MIDDLE EASTERN VETERAN'S OWN STRUGGLES WITH HIS OWN COMMUNITY

"The impediment to action advances action. What stands in the way becomes the way."—*Marcus Aurelius*

It was a cold night in early 2000 as I sat inside a mosque after Friday prayer. I was waiting for a couple of friends and decided to hang out in the common area. Several chairs and tables were scattered across the room. It was noisy from the various conversations going on. There were all sorts of people, from religious scholars to regular worshippers.

My attention was drawn to a conversation next to me. *"If you ain't a Muslim you deserve to die."* Two men were arguing. One was dressed in traditional Middle Eastern attire with a bushy beard. We will call him "Mr. Radical." He was very passionate about the subject being discussed. *No, brother that isn't right. So, you're telling me it doesn't matter your race, gender...?"* Mr. Radical quickly cut the man off and responded with, *I don't care if you're black, white, Asian, purple, green... if you ain't a Muslim you deserve to die."* Of course, this went against everything that I learned about Islam and the teachings of peace and love.

I left and told my parents what I had just heard. They brushed it off that Mr. Radical was a crazy guy and not to worry about it. This was pre- 9/11, I had just graduated high school and started college. My mind was focused on partying, girls, and more partying.

During my time in high school, I became friends with Ahmad Abu Samra. My parents were friends of his. His father was a respectable doctor. He was a funny kid, smart, and a good friend at the time. Slowly through the years, I started to see a change in him and changes in some of the other guys at the mosque. Ahmed, and a few other friends, would go to the mosque every Friday for prayer. My parents would drop me off so I could hang out with them. Ahmed started to dress in traditional Islamic attire. He became a lot more vocal toward non- Muslims. Someone at the mosque got to him. You could feel it, during the Friday night prayers. I could tell there were certain individuals looking to recruit. I started to distance myself from them. I knew something wasn't right.

As the years went by, I lost contact with Ahmed and some of the guys from the mosque. I learned that Ahmed went to Afghanistan and tried to join the Taliban. He then attempted to conduct a terrorist operation in the U.S. He tried targeting a mall but was unsuccessful. He was eventually charged by the FBI with federal terrorism charges.

We had similar upbringings but took different paths. All it took for Ahmed to go down his path was speaking to the wrong person. That person poisoned his mind. Some people are not born with a moral compass. They need to be told what to do, what laws to follow, follow the 10 commandments, etc. I am not one of those. I am not swayed by the media, social media memes, talking heads on the news, or religious figures.

So, how did it end for Ahmed? He left for Syria and joined ISIS. Ahmed became their social media guy. He was the one that made those disgusting videos of people being burned alive, beheaded, etc. His family had cut him off. He did not have any contact with anyone in the U.S., that I knew of, and was eventually killed in a U.S. airstrike.

Good riddance.

I moved on with my life. I graduated high school and went right into college. During my time in college, I did what most typical college students did. Partied, went to class and then partied again. Even with all that, I felt this sense of duty in me. I couldn't place it. I've always admired warriors, from the ancient ones to the modern warriors. They had honor, integrity, courage, and many more traits I admired.

On September 11, 2001, I woke up and got ready for school. I headed out and arrived shortly before 9:00 am. I watched as hundreds of students left the school, and I asked what was going on. One student told me we were attacked as a nation, and the faculty told the students to go home. I got home, and my family was huddled around the TV, watching the footage of the Twin Towers in New York. We watched the President of the United States declare war. It was a surreal time in America. Nearly every American I saw was waving a US Flag. It was as if the terrorist attack had awoken the sleeping giant again.

As the days and months went on, I had this itch in me. I wanted to join the fight. My reasons were much deeper than most. My reasons was to deploy and separate the good Muslims from the bad. My reason was to bridge that gap between Americans and those from the Middle East. I wanted to show that not all of us are bad.

As the months passed, I told my family I wanted to join the military. They were very much against it. That was understandable because the nation was at war, and they knew exactly where

I would end up. Their other reason was that I was going to fight fellow Muslims. To them, that was a huge NO.

Community members started catching on and scolding me for wanting to join. One day, my mother was having coffee with a friend of hers. Her friend looked at me sternly and said, "SO YOU WANT TO JOIN THE ENEMY."

I was shocked by that comment because she lives in the US and enjoys the freedoms we are given, and secondly, my mother did not come to my defense, and I remember feeling betrayed. It was at that moment I realized I was alone.

I returned to college one day, and several military recruiters were in the dining hall. I went to the first one, the US Army National Guard. For a couple of reasons, part of me wanted to appease the community by joining the guard because it meant I'll be home. The second reason, they had a great college program. So I joined and signed the dotted line. I didn't care what my parents thought or what the community thought. I had my reasons beyond anything they could comprehend.

My first introduction to the military was at the Military Entrance Processing Station (MEPS) in downtown Boston. My God was that an introduction. Fellow veterans will understand that statement because it was quite the experience. We were all briefed by this doctor wearing standard issue S9 Eyeglasses, affectionately known to male military members as BCGs or Birth Control Glasses because they are so ugly that no woman would want to have sex with you if she saw you wearing them.

This doctor started talking about barbiturates. I have no idea why, but he kept seeing that we would all undergo a drug test and we'd better not have barbiturates in our system. We were all snickering, standing there in just our underwear. It made us wonder if that doctor was on barbiturates.

After we were poked, prodded, and tested, we were given a "green" status, which means we were ready to join the armed forces. An enlisted soldier led us into a room with the US flag and every branch flag. We raised our right hand and swore our oath:

"I, Ayman Kafel, do solemnly swear that I will support and defend the Constitution of the United States against all enemies, foreign and domestic; that I will bear true faith and allegiance to the same; and that I will obey the orders of the President of the United States and the orders of the officers appointed over me, according to the regulations and the Uniform Code of Military Justice. So help me God."

My recruiter told me that the only opening they had was in Field Artillery, so me being young and dumb and not knowing any better, I went along with what the recruiter said, plus it looked cool to blow stuff up.

On September 12, 2002, I went to US Army Basic Training at Fort Sill, Oklahoma. I was assigned to Charlie Battery 1/40 1st platoon Warlords. I was there for three months because I was in a program called OSUT, which stands for One Station Unit Training. It combines both Basic Training and Advanced Individual Training (AIT).

Arriving at my barracks wearing those
dreaded BCGs.

I was alone and without family support. It was tough for me to leave home and go somewhere that was not familiar to me or my family. None of my family have ever served in any armed forces.

I remember making some phone calls home and received only a handful of letters. Even with those letters and phone calls, I still felt I was alone.

After months of blood, sweat, and tears, I finally finished my training, and graduation was a couple of weeks away. The drill sergeants gave us directions to relay to our families on how to obtain tickets for the graduation, hotels in the area, and other information.

I called home and spoke with my father. He told me he would not attend my graduation, nor would anyone else in the family. So again, I was alone. Finally, I got used to the idea.

I graduated in January 2003 and went home. There was no fanfare, no welcome home, just business as usual. I was assigned to the 102nd Field Artillery Company in Massachusetts. On my first day there, I was a young private. I didn't know anyone there, but they quickly welcomed me. After that, I became part of a brotherhood.

After several months of weekends and two-week duties with the National Guard, we received our orders to active duty. We were given orders to deploy to Iraq. I thought to myself, FINALLY!

2

WELCOME TO "MORTAR CITY" AND THE PRAETORIANS

"What's it all about?? Kicking Ass" — COL Dan McElroy

A C-130 Transport Plane lands in Camp Anaconda. The base is affectionately known as "mortar city" due to the constant mortar attacks that occur on the base. We land in the middle of the night. We get to a large briefing tent. A sergeant first class (SFC) greets us in the tent after we all sit down. He yells out, "WELCOME TO CAMP ANACONDA! OTHERWISE KNOWN AS MORTAR CITY." He continues briefing us regarding in- processing procedures and billeting. We process in and get to our temporary housing, a bunch of tents and cots. I lay on my cot, staring at the tent "ceiling", and slowly drift off to sleep.

BOOM! BOOM! BOOM! I woke up to the sounds of explosions. Air sirens were going off, the base was under mortar attack. My tent mates and I rushed from our tents to the safety of nearby bunkers. As we stood there huddled in the bunker, which wasn't even underground, I realized if a mortar hit us head-on, we would be dead anyway. This was a reality we just accepted at that point.

A few days later, a convoy of Humvees (gun trucks) with an M2, "the Ma Deuce" .50 caliber machine gun mounted arrived to pick us up. It took several convoys to get the entire company to our Forward Operating Base (FOB). As we traveled along the road, I saw different areas where Improvised Explosive Devices (IEDs) had exploded. I could hear pockets of gunfire at different points of the convoy.

At last, we got to the FOB and finally settled into our tents. Each soldier was able to get some sort of mattress for the cots. We built makeshift walls for privacy. Each tent housed anywhere from 10 to 15 soldiers. We were fortunate to be on a FOB that was in open desert as this made it very difficult for anyone to attempt to mortar or attack us. The company was given its mission for the year.

A few days later the company commander (CO CMDR) had to go into Baghdad for a meeting at an embassy. I was tasked to go with the squad of soldiers that were escorting him. We arrived in Baghdad and made our way to the gates of the embassy, which was guarded by the Iraqi Army. The squad leader asked for my help to translate. I dismounted from the gun truck and began issuing orders to the Iraqi Army soldiers. At first, they were confused. I'm sure they thought: "Wait, is this American soldier speaking Arabic?? What is going on here??" a few seconds later the gates were opened, and we were led in. A few of the Iraqi soldiers walked up to me and we all shook hands.

At an embassy in Baghdad.

We exchanged pleasantries to the point that the squad was offered water, juice, and snacks. The squad leader immediately turned to me and said, "Sergeant, you are an asset." I eventually told the squad members to keep their eyes on the Iraqi soldiers. The squad felt comfortable knowing that I understood Arabic and would warn the men if there were any danger. After a couple of hours, the CO CMDR came out, we loaded up in the gun trucks, and headed back to our FOB.

A couple of weeks later, I was given a new mission. I was assigned to the Battalion Commander's (BN CMDR) personal security detail (PSD). The squad was called "Praetorians". They were named after an elite unit within the Roman Army whose members served as the personal bodyguards for the Roman Emperor. The BN CMDR's call sign was "Spartan 6." After my deployment, I found our call signs quite fitting. We were a small squad of soldiers who traveled all over northern Iraq with a BN CMDR that never slept and conducted over 30,000 miles of combat patrols.

Our BN CMDR was not afraid to kick in a door when it was necessary, and our squad covered his six at all times. I reported to the BN CMDR. He is slightly shorter than I am, but he has command presence and a type of energy that made his soldiers just want to run into battle with him. One thing I learned from him about being a leader is to talk to a subordinate as one of your own. He shook my hand, we shared a few laughs, and proceeded to meet the rest of the Praetorians.

I met the Praetorian squad leader (SQ LDR). He looked like he hadn't slept in ages. I guess that happens when a squad leader is responsible for the well-being of the BN CMDR; the squad is always on the move and the members get very little sleep. The SQ LDR introduced me to the rest of the Praetorians, as they were cleaning their weapons preparing for the next mission.

All of them welcomed me as one of their own. That's one thing I loved about the military. It didn't matter where you were from, what color your skin was, or your what religion you followed. "We all bleed green" is the motto. I saw it first-hand. The only thing that ever mattered was the soldiers to your left and right. That's it.

Praetorians and Spartan 6 at the Saddam Swords in Baghdad.

After few minutes of getting to know each other, we were given our mission by the SQ LDR. I went back to my tent to prepare. I realized it was going to be an extremely busy time for me. I was also anxious. Here I was, 23-years-old, and had to ensure my situational awareness was at 100% at all times. Eleven men relied on me to assess a situation and give them the information needed so we could respond appropriately. I also had to make sure I didn't give up any information about where I was from or who my family was. I still had family in Lebanon, which was a short hop from Iraq. Interpreters were always hunted down by Al-Qaeda terrorists. A soldier who spoke Arabic. That was worth ten times more to Al-Qaeda.

3

CAUGHT BETWEEN CULTURES

It was in the middle of the night in the cold Iraqi desert. It sounds funny to say "cold desert." At any rate, the Praetorians and Spartan 6 were conducting a combat patrol during an Iraqi election. Every time an election came around in Iraq, it was met with violence and intimidation from various terrorist groups throughout the country. Our mission that night was to ensure the ballots made it through our area of operations (AO) without any problems.

One of the gunners informed us that there was someone down the road digging at the side of the road. As we moved toward him, he ran off. We gave chase but lost him in one of the local villages. We ended up clearing all the mud huts in the village. As we went through each hut, I would order the occupants to keep their hands where we could see them. Unfortunately, we were unable to find this person. We went back to the area where we initially saw him and saw the Improvised Explosive Device (IED) he had been assembling. It was safe to be close to it since it hadn't been completed. We called in an Explosive Ordinance and Disposal (EOD) unit to get rid of the device.

Praetorian on guard.

I walked around with my fellow Praetorians as Spartan 6 was talking with the prison warden near Mosul. I kept my eyes and ears on the Iraqi Police (IP) walking with the warden and Spartan 6. Spartan 6 was using a local interpreter at the time, and I purposely kept quiet just in case I was able to gain any intel from unsuspecting IPs that didn't know I spoke Arabic. A male subject walked by me and I noticed there was a pistol, looked like a Glock to me, hidden at the small of his back. The butt of the pistol was sticking out. I walked behind him, yelling out to him in Arabic "STOP. DO NOT MOVE ANOTHER STEP." He froze in his tracks. I told him to drop the gun and step back or I would I shoot him. He complied. The warden quickly shouted that the male subject was one of his IPs. He was part of his protective detail.

Could that have been a possible attempted assassination of Spartan 6? Was the IP an Al-Qaeda Terrorist that made it into the IPs? So many questions were going through my head. He was eventually identified and let go.

There were times I suspected certain Iraqis I spoke with were there to do more harm than good. I found it frustrating that the Iraqis did not have a concept of fighting for their country. They would fight for a religious figure, dictator, or ideology. They did not understand the concept of persons of mixed races and religions fighting for each other and their country.

One day, while we were talking to some Iraqis, I pointed out that our whole squad was made up of people from all races and religions. I explained that we fought for each other and our country.

Talking to Iraqi Police Officers.

I was asked several times by the Iraqis why I joined the U.S. military. My response was always the same: "I JOINED TO HELP SEPARATE THE BAD ARABS FROM THE GOOD ONES." It's something I needed to do when the U.S. went to war in the Middle East. I knew my country needed someone like me, because American service members were about to step into a world that would be tough to understand.

Laughing with some Iraqis.

I called home one day and spoke to my sister. She told me that this man in a pick-up truck tried to run my mother off the road. She dresses in traditional Middle Eastern clothing and has a thick accent. A thought flashed through my mind: "Why the hell am I out here fighting for a country that doesn't care about my culture." I was angry that I faced backlash over joining the U.S. Military and fighting in the Middle East within the Middle Eastern community. To me, I was surrounded by "enemies" on both sides of the pond. Whether the enemy was racism or terrorism, I was surrounded by it. Racism wasn't just from a fellow American but also from those from within the Middle Eastern community. Mind you, at my time in war, I was a green card holder and not a U.S. Citizen yet. It wasn't until a few years later, after Immigration and Naturalization Service (INS) found my lost file, that I became a U.S. Citizen.

A memory: my squad drives along MSR (main supply route) Dover, en route to Camp Anaconda. I am standing in the gunner's position, wearing my face mask and goggles. Dust hits my face and uniform as the sweat from the desert heat trickles down my face and back. I'm wearing 50-pound IBA (individual body armor) with extra ammo, my M-16 right next to me in case my trusty M2 .50 caliber machine gun fails. We approach a one-lane bridge.

The Iraqi Army has stopped both sides of traffic. My squad stops to assess the situation. Our battalion commander wants me to tell the Iraqi soldier standing next to my truck that we need to move. I speak with the soldier in Arabic. The Iraqi soldier looks perplexed as if I was somehow speaking a foreign language that he understood. He replies in Arabic, I don t speak English." So, I respond, again in Arabic, and say: Well how about we speak Arabic then?" The Iraqi soldier nods in agreement as a smile spread across his face.

The above was one of many encounters I experienced in Iraq. The Iraqis were used to dealing with civilian translators with U.S. Soldiers. But they never got used to an American soldier speaking Arabic, who understood their culture. Every time I encountered an Iraqi, they would first tell me that they didn't understand. They just couldn't believe a U.S. Soldier was speaking Arabic, let alone a U.S. Soldier who was also from the Middle East.

What was it like for me to enlist? I was met with fierce opposition from my local Middle Eastern community. I was called everything from the enemy to a traitor, to a bad son, to a bad example for the younger generations. I heard about fathers going to religious figures in the community asking for advice for their sons so they wouldn't "end up like me." All this did was fuel the fire in me even more. I ended up enlisting in the National Guard. I chose to serve part-time for two reasons: I wanted to graduate college and wanted to to try to appease the worries of my local community by being able to be there at least some of the time.

As I wrote in the previous chapter, at boot camp, I was alone and didn't get many letters from home. When I was allowed phone calls, they were brief and awkward. During the final weeks of boot camp and AIT, we were given our graduation dates. I called home and informed my family when I was going to graduate. I was told that no one was coming. I knew that might happen. I graduated and went home with no fanfare, no family congratulating me. It was back to normal.

A year and a half later, I got my orders to go to war. I was both scared and excited at the same time. My family, on the other hand, was not happy, understandably so. What parents want to see their child off to war? I also dealt with the backlash from my family and community. At this point, I knew what to expect from them. They would not understand why I had to go. For me, it was my duty to go and fight. It was about my fellow soldiers out there. It was also about protecting those who were not part of that fight. I knew my language and cultural awareness would be helpful to my unit and the civilians I would encounter.

I PREPARE FOR
THE DAY

My mind focused.

My determination directed. My resolve strengthened.

My primal instincts enhanced.

*The sounds of iron hitting the floor sounds like a battle of the
ancients.*
My heart beats as if it is beating the drums of war.
*This is what I have become, what I am, where I am the most comfort-
able.*

Screams of pain echo in my head.
Remind me of a time I first greeted death.
Beads of sweat from my forehead are a reminder of
the hardships I have endured and what I will endure.
*This is what I have become, what I am, where I am the most comfort-
able.*

I slip on my gear.
Radio check.
Weapons locked and loaded.

Mission brief.

It s time to greet death once again.
It s time to play that game we always play.

4

THE DAY I GOT KICKED OUT OF THE ARMY

"Difficulties strengthens the mind, as labor does the body." —Seneca

There is a part of me that will always, no matter what, think about the worst day of my life. Sure, picking up body parts of a fellow soldier after an IED strike was awful. Witnessing the horrors mankind inflicts upon itself during war is awful. Being a cop is always awful. The lifeless corpse of a child who was neglected by parents is awful. Despite all this, what was the worst day of my life? The day I got kicked out of the military like some piece of trash with a medical discharge.

This was in 2008. The unit I was a part of was ramping up to go to Iraq. This would have been my second deployment. There are always requirements to be completed at the unit level before any deployment. Some of the requirements involve medical, administrative, training, and so forth. Once the unit completes all these necessary tasks, they can deploy.

I was in Iraq in 2005. During my deployment, my gun truck was struck head-on by a civilian motor vehicle moving at a high rate of speed. I don't remember much of that day. When the vehicle struck my truck, I was knocked out. When I regained consciousness, the interior of the truck was filled with smoke. I thought we'd been struck by an IED, so I felt around to make sure I had all my limbs. I yelled out, "HEY DID WE GET HIT BY AN IED??"

My gunner yelled out, "NO, IT WAS A CAR." I stepped out of the truck and secured the area while we waited for reinforcements to arrive. We weren't in the best area. Eventually, we got back to the FOB and reported to the medics. I had a large bump on my head and some back pain. Typical for the Army, I got some Motrin and a "have a nice day." In hindsight, even if they had told me I needed a MEDEVAC (medical evacuation) to a hospital at one of our major bases, I would have refused. I would not leave my squad. Squad mates treating the driver of the car that hit us

The next injury was a torn meniscus (MCL). That was my fault. Being the stupid young soldier that I was, I jumped out of the back of a 5-ton, with all my gear, and felt the pop when I landed. I should have dumped my gear and then jumped down. So, once again I reported to the medics. They checked my knee, I was in pain, and most likely had a torn MCL. If I required treatment, I'd have to leave and go to Germany. This NCO was not going anywhere. My response was "FUCK NO, GIVE ME SOME MOTRIN AND A KNEE WRAP."

Squad mates treating the driver of the car that hit us.

I finished my deployment and came home. Over 40,000 miles of combat patrols, missions, etc. I had felt every mile. I ended up getting knee surgery and then worked on my back. I had an MRI and found out that my L5 disc was touching my S1 nerve. It was extremely painful. I wanted to avoid surgery, so I went with several treatment options.

During that time, I became a cop. I aced the police academy physical fitness standards. I knocked the yearly Army PT test out of the park while undergoing treatment. During the police academy, I got a hair-line fracture on my right foot. I had to wear a cast. For a week, I watched my fellow academy mates get smoked, running multiple miles every day. Against doctor's orders, I took off my cast and ran 5 miles with my academy mates. One comment that was made by the drill instructors during graduation, "YOU'RE PROBABLY ONE OF THE MOST MOTIVATED GUYS I'VE EVER MET."

I'd been a cop for about a year when my National Guard unit received orders to go back to Iraq in 2008. So, here we go again. It was time to go through the process of going to war. During the ramp-up, I went through medical tests and listed some of the medications I was on due to my back pain. A medic sergeant decided to question me further on one of the medications, which was a very mild pain killer. From one NCO to another, the sergeant questioned how I could handle a weapon while on the medication. I told the medic I was fine, that I was also an active law enforcement officer and that none of my medications inhibited my ability to perform.

The sergeant wasn't having any of it. I was immediately recommended to go before a Medical Evaluation Board (MEB). The MEB is a process designed to determine whether a Service member's long-term medical condition enables him/her to continue to meet medical retention standards, in accordance with military service regulations. It also provides an opportunity for military physicians to clearly document all care and treatments received prior to MEB referral and any duty limitations their condition may cause.

The MEB is considered an informal board because, by itself, it does not drive any personnel actions. The findings of the MEB are referred to the Physical Evaluation Board (PEB), which formally determines fitness for continued service and eligibility for disability compensation. The MEB is convened once the medical retention decision point is reached or when the Service member's physician thinks the Service member will not be able to return to duty for medical reasons. The board evaluates a Service member's medical history and condition, documents the extent of the injury or illness, and decides whether the Service member's medical condition is severe enough to impede his/her ability to continue serving in a full duty capacity.

Entering into the MEB process does not mean the Service member will be automatically discharged from military service. The MEB will refer a Service member to the PEB when the findings and recommendations stipulate that either:

- the Service member does not meet retention standards, or
- the Service member should return to duty in a different military occupation specialty (MOS).

MEB decisions can affect the Service member and family, so it is necessary for all to understand the entire board process. Having all the documents and necessary medical information completed before the board meets is vital to achieving the best outcome. The MEB recommended that I be medically discharged. I was angry and hurt at the same time. I wanted to deploy with my unit. The worst feeling was that, my platoon already knew I was being discharged. While in formation, I heard a comment, "YOU'RE PROBABLY THE BEST NCO WE'VE EVER HAD." It gave me much pride even as it stung to have to leave. I couldn't deploy with my brothers-in-arms.

But I stayed behind.

After that, I was overcome with depression, anger, and everything in between. I said to myself, "fuck it all." A couple of years later, friends of mine, who were working at the HQ level asked why I hadn't reach out to them for help. They could've stopped the med board from kicking me out. My response was, why would I try to stay in an Army that would toss you aside in a heartbeat. I went to war; if the Army didn't expect me to come back with a single injury, then they were seriously disconnected from the realities of the soldiers on the ground.

In the end, I did not decide I wanted to get out. It was forced onto me. I was not prepared to leave yet. I wanted to deploy, not because I love war, but for love of my brothers. I wanted to deploy because of the brand-new privates in the unit. I wanted to make sure they got the best training to prepare them for what they were about to have to do. That was the worst day of my life. The day I got kicked out of the Army.

The day I couldn't be there with my guys.

5

SURVIVORS' GUILT

"It is not death that a man should fear, but rather he should fear never beginning to live." —Marcus Aurelius

It was a pleasant September day in 2005. The Praetorians were getting ready for their patrol. This time, we had another squad with us. Out of respect for the squad, I will not reveal their unit or other squad members. Instead, I will refer to them as *"Spartan QRF."* QRF stands for Quick Reaction Force. A QRF squad is always on standby and ready to receive orders from the BN CMDR. Their orders could span from repelling an assault to conducting convoy security.

On September 20, 2005, they joined us on patrol outside the wire. We received our mission brief from the BN CMDR. We mounted, conducted a weapons check, and went outside the wire. We decided to go in different directions so we could cover more ground. At some point, we reversed direction. We were supposed to go left, and Spartan QRF went right. At the last second, we went right, and they went left.

A few minutes later, we hear a frantic call for help, we hear a MEDEVAC get called in. *Spartan QRF* struck an IED. A rather large one. We race to get to them. I remember getting there and seeing the chaos. Soldiers were running around frantically trying to get their comrades out of the gun trucks.

Spartan QRF Gun truck after being struck by an IED.

I was tasked with ensuring the BN CMDR had communication with air support and the Battalion Tactical Operations Center (TOC). My body just went into automatic mode. There is a popular saying amongst warriors that states "your training takes over when under duress." If you take your training seriously you will rise to the occasion. If you don't take it your training seriously then you will fail. At this moment, I thank God I took my training seriously.

Once the radios were set, I step out of the BN CMDR gun truck and made my way to the scene. The smell of death, screams of pain, anger, rage filled the air. The MEDEVAC Blackhawk landed and we starting evacuating the killed and wounded soldiers.

After the dust settled and the wounded were evacuated, we all sat for a moment. I remember seeing my BN CMDR seated on a mound talking with air support. We had an Apache gunship provide us cover while we assessed the scene.

The Praetorians started collecting the body parts of the soldier who was killed. I found a large piece of the soldier about 100 meters from the blast site. One of my squad mates started dry heaving when I picked up the large piece. I told him to walk away. We placed his body parts in a cooler in the BN CMDRs truck.

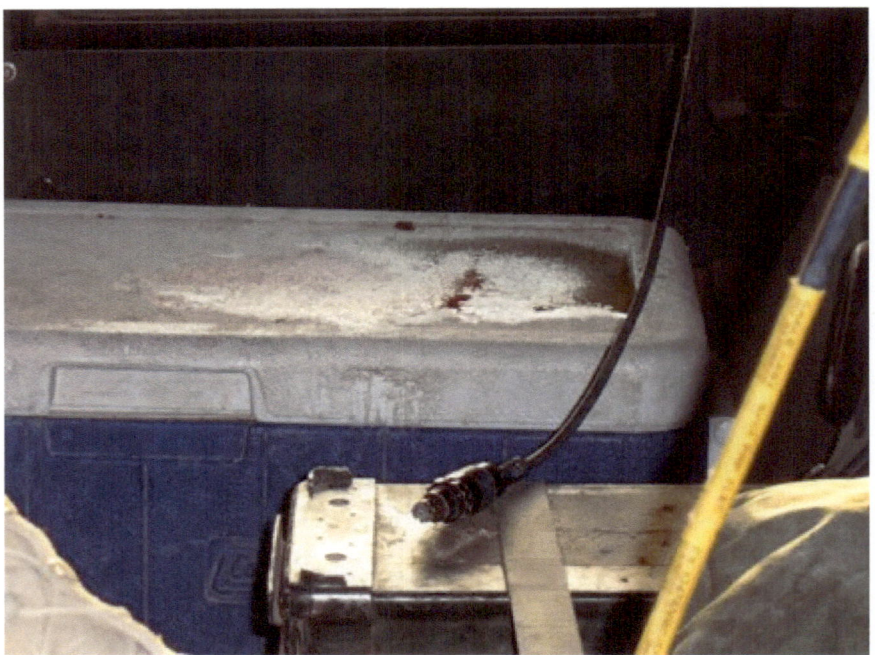

Soldier's body parts next to me.

In the days proceeding, a memorial was held, and a crisis team came out to speak to the squad. The crisis team was a new thing in the Army where if a soldier was involved in a critical incident, a group of psychologists and counselors came out and spoke to the involved soldiers. Most of us stayed quiet about the incident. We didn't know if they would force us to go home if we did speak up.

In November of 2005, the Battalion spearheaded an operation where High-Value Targets (HVTs) were wanted, and we were tasked with capturing them.

There were weeks of planning, training, and coordinating with different units. At zero dark thirty, the mission kicked off. As units were approaching the objective, a gun truck was struck by an IED. I initially thought, "Oh no, here we go again." We raced to the blast's location and saw the chaos again. The remaining units were ordered to continue the mission and hit the objective of capturing the HVTs.

A medic was working on a soldier who was critically wounded. I will never forget the sounds he made while gasping for air. MEDEVAC landed and took the wounded soldier. The mission was accomplished, but with the cost of a soldier who died at the hospital table.

Again, like before, memorials were held, the crisis unit came, and then we were back at running missions. One question lingered in me, why did I survive? The two soldiers who died before my eyes had a family, had young children, so again I asked, why did I survive. It is a question that remains with me to this day. I even learned what it was called. It's called *"Survivors' Guilt."*

When I came home, I decided to volunteer in the Massachusetts Army National Guard Honor Guard. I felt that I owed it to the veterans who paid that ultimate sacrifice to honor them.

OCTOBER 28, 2007   BOSTON SUNDAY GLOBE

MASS. SOLDIER REMEMBERED — An honor guard carried the casket of Army Private First Class Kenneth Iwasinski during his funeral yesterday in Belchertown. Iwasinski, 22, was killed Oct. 14 when his vehicle was hit by an improvised explosive device in Iraq. At right are his father and stepmother, Dominick and Tawnia.

The MA National Guard Honor Guard. I am up front and on the right.

Photo by Christopher Evans

It was a difficult mission but an honorable one. We were so careful and so methodical on how we conducted ourselves. We not only honored the soldier but also the family. One of the most difficult parts was when it came to the folding of the flag. There is a silence. You can hear the quiet cries of the family. As I folded every section of the flag, I felt the hurt that the family felt. As I folded every section of the flag. My memories flooded with those we lost while I was there. My question came back again, why did I survive? What purpose am I still here for?

A lot of combat veterans suffer from survivors' guilt. A lot of personal friends of mine share stories of how they missed something or didn't report something and soldiers died as a result. It's a guilt that haunts us more than anything else. It's the demon that stays on our shoulders and reminds us of our survival. It reminds us of our struggle.

FOR THE STRUGGLING VETERAN

At times
It's not about
Physical strength

But strengthening your mind
At times
It's not about
Physical therapy

But mental therapy
Wake up
Self-assess
Conquer your demons

Through sweat and steel

Dig deep
We are warriors
It's what we do

Most don't understand
But we do
Stay on Azimuth
Charlie Mike...

6

WINNING THE BATTLE AT HOME: TRANSFORMING ANGER INTO MOTIVATION

"Out of suffering have emerged the strongest souls; the most massive characters are seared with scars."— *Kahlil Gibran*

January of 2006, my flight home from Iraq came up fast! Of course, like every other combat veteran, I was scared shitless of my last couple of weeks of operations. Any combat veteran will tell you that the last month of deployment is the most dangerous. It's because complacency sets in, looking forward to going home, making plans, etc. When our plane finally took off to go home, there was loud applause on the plane. Finally, heading home.

Our first leg home was landing in Dublin, Ireland. We had a long layover so the plane could be refueled and refit with supplies for the rest of the flight. Bars were open, and we were allowed to grab a drink. As you can imagine, it wasn't just one drink. It was several. We all stumbled back on the plane, and I slept the rest of the ride home. We landed in Ft Dix, NJ. Another loud applause from the company. We really made it!

We got to our barracks and downloaded our gear. The next few days were much downtime and getting out-processed from deployment, otherwise known as DEMOB. At one point, the entire unit had to go to a briefing held by the VA. At one point during the briefing, one of the VA reps said to us, "If you don't feel ok or need some help, please tell us. We are here to help you. Once you tell one of the counselors that you need help, you will remain on base while we conduct an assessment." Do you think anyone was going to admit that they were having issues? Only one soldier admitted he was having issues, and while we all went home, he stayed on base. We later learned that he was placed in a platoon of soldiers who were deserters, injured, or not fit for combat duty. He was treated like crap by the command of that unit. Do you think that soldier became better? Nope. He got worse. We lost contact with him eventually. I only hope he got better.

We arrive at our home station a couple of weeks later. There were friends and family waiting. Big signs welcoming us home. It was nice. I get off the bus and get a ride home. I didn't tell my family that I was coming home. I wanted to surprise them. I get home and knock on the door. My brothers and sisters answered the door, and the house ignited excitement. I was finally home.

This is the point where things started to go wrong...

I felt out of place. I felt on edge. I felt no purpose. My sister tells me, which I have no memory of that she would come to check on me late at night, and I'd sit on my bed staring at the blank wall in front of me. I would sit on the couch, and the TV would be off, and stare at the screen. One night she turned on the TV and sat with me all night.

I do remember driving around my town, and one day, I remember this car behind me tailgating me. The woman driver was honking and giving me that good old middle finger. I remember looking at my speedometer and seeing that I was traveling the speed limit. I have no clue what I could have done to be subject to such aggression. My anger just skyrocketed. All I thought was that I had two soldiers get killed right in front of me a month or two prior, and this is what I come home to.

I slammed my brakes and got out of the car with a bat I had in the trunk. The lady took off in horror because I could only imagine the look I had on my face. My son says, "You have murder eyes when you get mad." So I guess that was the look. I'm surprised I didn't get the cops called on me, or if I did, they didn't follow up with me.

As the weeks progressed, my anger got worse. Anything would set me off, from my minor pet peeves to not remembering why I got mad. I remember I would argue with my siblings, just everyday sibling bullshit, but at some point, I'd snap and punch holes in walls, throw chairs and furniture around, and whatever was within my reach, it would break. My bedroom had so many holes that my father hired a contractor to redo the walls.

In retrospect, I was thinking back. I was trained to use extreme violence and aggression when combating the enemy. The Army never taught me how to turn that side off. This was all I knew. I perceive a threat, and I act in kind. I react with Speed, Surprise, and Violence of Action.

Before I get into this next story, I feel it may be necessary to re-explain my feelings about my family and community. I grew up in a Muslim household, we escaped civil war in Lebanon and Liberia, and my parents were unhappy that I joined the US Army. Community members called me a traitor, and my parents did not stand up for me. I had to do it all myself. So, this next story will be understood by those who have read my articles.

I was helping with the dishes one day. My mother asked me about my time in Iraq, and I did not want to talk about it because I was uncomfortable talking to them. At one point, I'll never forget this. She says, "YOU KNOW IF YOU KILL A MUSLIM, YOU GO TO HELL."

I don't remember my response or what I did. I most likely blanked out with rage again and broke something.

My father, out of nowhere, wanted to meet me to meet him at a coffee shop with my uncle. He asked me why I was so angry. My only response was, are you kidding me? Do you know where I have been? What I have been through? I wanted to open up, but I knew it would not have gotten anywhere because of my previous conversations with them and how I was treated when I joined the Army.

A few months go by, and I'm still angry, still without purpose. I had nowhere to channel this rage that was developed in me, The Lion suddenly awoke. This Lion was held in a cage by modern-day society but is now unleashed. I felt insane. "Insanity is coasting through life in a miserable existence when you have a caged lion locked inside and the key to release it." One of my favorite quotes was said by Morgan Freeman in the movie Wanted.

The police exam came up. I decided to take it. I needed purpose. I needed a new mission. I needed to feel like I was a part of something much bigger than myself. I remember sitting at a desk at my old job, staring at the wall. I finally concluded that I was wasting away. Listening to civilians bitch and moan about the most minor things. These same civilians, when I went back to work, said to me, "YOU LOOK LIKE YOU'VE BEEN THROUGH HELL." No shit, I thought. Where do you think I've been for the last 18 months?

I took the exam, passed it, and was in the Police Academy a year later. During the process, I was treated the same way by my family. The same crap, the same language of disappointment. My mother said, "I WILL NEVER SUPPORT YOU." I figured it would be like that.

Here is the thing, I decided to channel that anger and make it productive for me. I decided to convert that anger into a type of determination that would push me to limits I didn't know I had. I pushed beyond those limits. I kept pushing myself to excel. To be the best I can be. My anger turned into determination, resilience, and resolve. Nothing could stop me from achieving my goals. Nothing. As I mentioned earlier in this book, when I injured my foot during my academy training, I couldn't run for a few weeks as a result. I was in a cast and sat on the sidelines as my platoon would get smoked and run over 5 miles. I felt bad. So, I decided, about a week or so later, I would take off my cast and ran with my platoon. It was that drive that I had developed, that warrior spirit. That Lion was uncaged.

I graduated from the academy, and it was a proud moment for me. My family got to pin my badge. My father and uncle were invited, and my dad was supposed to pin me. I said supposed to because he showed up late and after the ceremony had concluded. Do you know who ended up pinning me? A family friend I had invited. I was both embarrassed and disappointed. Yet again, like graduating boot camp, I didn't have my family in my corner. So, I was still alone and angry.

In the end, what I've learned is to channel that anger into something positive. The things I have accomplished are not because of family support. It was because of my own self-taught drive. This drive in me that continues to pump is a part of me. This anger is a part of me that I've learned to channel. That's my message to every service member, fellow veterans, and police officers. Use that drive. Make it productive and not destructive. I don't know where I would be if I continued down the path of destruction.

7

I CAME BACK... BUT NOT REALLY

"For whatever trauma came with service in tough circumstances, we should take what we learned - take our post-traumatic growth - and, like past generations coming home, bring our sharpened strengths to bear, bring our attitude of gratitude to bear." —*General James Mattis*

June is PTSD awareness month. There is a lot of craziness in the world right now. I thought I'd share mine. There are so many veterans who are suffering every day. Veterans across the country commit suicide every day. The Veterans Affairs (VA) has come a long way, but still has a lot of work to do to address PTSD. It truly is the invisible wound that no one sees. A lot of veterans do a good job hiding it. After all, we are "heroes". Veterans have a hard time reaching out because of how many times the systems in place have failed us. Just look at how many stories there are of veterans wanting to die, whether it's suicide by cop or other means. I watched this video on YouTube. It was a news story about a struggling veteran and a police officer who happens to be a combat veteran.

This video was tough for me to watch. The veteran wanted to commit suicide. I felt the pain in both. One as a veteran who is also a cop and as a veteran. The police officer managed to get the veteran to drop the gun he was holding, and they ended up embracing one another as brothers.

A few years ago, I had to deal with an unstable veteran, on the verge of suicide. He was in my cruiser, and I took him to the local psychiatric hospital to be admitted. He was a Marine who saw his fair share of combat. His voice would break up here and there as he spilled his story to me. I had to keep strong for both of us because I saw the pain in his eyes. I've always hated seeing fellow veterans suffer the way they do. In the end, we have only each other.

My Story

The flight home from Iraq was uneventful. It was full of laughs and tired soldiers who just wanted to go home. We landed in Dublin, Ireland, for a quick stop to refuel. The company exited the plane to stretch our legs and walk around the terminal. The bars were open, so understandably, the soldiers were eager to grab a pint or two. Then I heard in the background the sound of glass breaking and someone, I assume the bartender, yelling out, "Fucking Americans." It made me chuckle a little. We got back on the flight and continued our trek home.

The plane landed at Fort Dix, New Jersey. The cheering was louder than the plane engines. We came to a stop and began making our way to our assigned barracks. I rested my head on my pillow in bed. I couldn't sleep. It was the same for the other soldiers. It all came flooding back. It had only been a couple of months since I witnessed the last IED strike against one of our soldiers. SSG Kyle Wherly (RIP) was KIA during an operation on November 6, 2005.

The next morning, we made our way to a briefing from a representative from Veterans Affairs. We learned that we were going to be on base for two weeks to re-acclimate to society. They pointed out that we were not the same. Everyone in the U.S. had moved on, while we were "stuck in time." One of the representatives said that if any of us were having a tough time to let them know. Then we learned that we would have to stay on base even longer if we said we were having issues. I thought, "Wow, great incentive!! Go home or stay on base." I went into the kiosk to talk to the VA rep and told him, "I'm good to go." We walked out of the briefing and made our way back to our barracks. A loud "BOOM" went off and my heart rate skyrocketed. I scanned the direction of the sound, and it was a tractor trailer bouncing over a speed bump. I took a quick deep breath and said to myself, "All clear."

Two weeks went by, and we all made it back home. I didn't tell my family I was coming home. I figured I'd surprise them and part of me didn't know if they would even show up if they did know. I got a ride with one of my battle buddies and he dropped me off at my house. It was late in the evening. I knocked on the door and was greeted with excitement. My brothers and sisters ran up to me to hug me. Same with my parents. After things settled down, I grabbed my gear and headed to my old room. My father had finished the basement. There was a full kitchen, full bathroom, living room, dining room and two bedrooms. I basically lived in my own place. I opened the door, and nothing had changed. Everything was still there. My Metallica posters, Pantera posters, banners, etc. Everything looked the same. I showered up and got myself ready for bed. I lay down. I couldn't sleep. Echoes of soldiers screaming rang in my head. Various sounds from Iraq stayed with me. I sat up, went to the living room, turned on the TV and sat on the couch. Before I knew it, it was morning.

About a couple of weeks went by, and it was more of the same. Hardly any sleep. Sitting in the living room. Watching TV, trying to make the time pass. I took melatonin, and that didn't work. I had some messed up dreams that forced me awake. One night (my sister told me this because I don't remember), my sister found me sitting up in my bed and staring at the wall in front of me. She got my attention, and we sat on the couch and watched movies.

Another couple of weeks went by. I could feel this rage inside me that I'd been trying to keep contained. It had been so difficult. My room, the walls were full of holes from the times I had punched them.

My anger then turned toward my family. My parents were useless and couldn't figure out why I was so angry. Partly, because of one of my conversations with them that went like this: "You know if you killed Muslims there, it is bad for you." That was said to me. That rage in me grew fiercely. The community called me all sorts of names. Civilian friends of mine were no longer friends. One of them said, "Man you've changed, dude." I wasn't that wild college kid doing weekend benders. I was reserved. I didn't want to go into bars, clubs, or anywhere that had a lot of people. I didn't like talking to civilians because of their bitching about the most trivial crap. One of my friends said to me, "You look like you've been through Hell over there." I realized I didn't like any of those labels. It made whatever I was going through real.

I went back to the old job I had during college, as a receptionist at a doctor's office. I sat behind a desk, taking phone calls and dealing with insurance companies. One day I just looked around and said to myself, "No, this is not me." I ended up taking the police exam and eventually became a cop.

It took me a long time to really face my demons. There are days I still struggle from memories that come back to me. Sometimes I think, "Holy fuck, it's nearly 20 years ago and shit still feels like it was yesterday." My VA therapist says that is very normal. Only recently have I really taken my therapy seriously. I thought I could just "medicate" my issues, but clearly that is more destructive. These days, my meds remind me that I am not the same. My medications remind me that I never really came home. As I told my family once, "That kid you guys knew, he died out there. This is who you have now."

So, brothers and sisters out there, I write this with hope that you read it and realize you are not alone. Please always ask for help when needed. Talk to a fellow veteran whom you served with or a veteran who served during a time of combat. Call the VA crisis line. Never ever think that suicide is the answer because it isn't. I know at times the "noise" gets to be too much. I've woken up saying to myself, "it's too noisy." I've woken up jumping out of my bed thinking a bomb went off or shots were fired. These things happen even now.

We have only each other. Let's help one another like we did while at war.

The things I have seen as a cop... well, that's a whole different conversation.

Have You Ever Wondered Who You'd Be Without War?

Have you ever wondered who you'd be without war? Seriously? I have thought about it quite a bit and, if I were given the choice, I'd do it all over again in a heartbeat.

Why? What was so great about it? Nothing. It sucked. It was what I earned, learned, and gained from it that will sustain me for the rest of my life.

The things I learned in war will help me teach my children and grandchildren. They will help me help other Vets recover. They will allow me to be the example of "greater love hath no man than to give up his life for his brothers." These are the things that make me who I am.

When you go to war, a part of you dies, and you are reborn like a Phoenix. You have more inner strength, fortitude, willpower, and resolve. You have all those qualities and more. General James Mattis said it best: PTSD is not a crippling disorder. Our experiences made us resilient and stronger than most. What you learn at war makes you appreciate life that much more. The small things do not get to you as much. You care more, you have seen the horrors man commits and know what man is capable of.

You come back with brothers. A set of different kinds of brothers. Brothers who spilled the same blood in the same mud. We laughed, cried, fought, and honored those we lost. That bond is something no one can ever fully understand.

Who did I become? I became more than a man. I rose out of the fire as a Phoenix re-born.

So, have you wondered who you'd be without war?

Think about it.

PART 2: THROUGH THE EYES OF A POLICE OFFICER

8

PREDATOR HUNTING PREDATORS

"Victorious warriors win first and then go to war, while defeated warriors go to war first and then seek to win."—Sun Tzu

The public goes about their day, to the mall, a movie theater, a baseball game, the beach, etc. Within that world, there is another world. A secret world. A world that is dangerous, volatile, and violent.

Around the corner, an unassuming man motions another to approach him...a drug deal occurs. Out of nowhere, several individuals in tactical gear surround both men and arrest them. They are gone as quickly as they appeared.

I described the cop who found the suspect in the crawl space. Why did that officer gravitate towards that area? Did he hear a sound? Or was it something deeper? Could the officer have smelled the testosterone of the suspect? Subconsciously, whether the officer knew it or not, he was drawn toward and found the crawl space because of that scent or sense There is a scientific theory behind this. According to a study conducted by Rockefeller University, androsterone, a derivative of testosterone that is a potent ingredient in male body odor, can be detected by olfactory senses in humans. A human, attuned to their environment, can pick up on certain smells, sounds, and senses, like a wolf dog.

Cops who have these traits end up in other specialty units, such as SWAT, Narcotics, Detectives, Street Crimes Units, Gang Units, and Fugitive Task Forces. Those jobs attract a certain breed of cops. They are combat veterans; they are cops who face impossible odds to save others. They work in the shadows; they aren't recognized for their work, nor do they want this. They are "silent professionals," among you "hunting" the wolves of society. They are constantly training, finding ways to perfect their skills, to keep themselves at the tip of the spear.

I'm by no means knocking the sheepdog officer. Each type of cop plays a vital part in our society and each job is important. What I am saying is that there are inherently two different kinds of cops.

"To protect the sheep, you have to catch the wolf and it takes a wolf to catch a wolf," said Denzel Washington's character in the movie *Training Day*. Why is that? Is it because the officer thinks like the wolf they are after? Do the wolves have this wild side in them that enables them to go after dangerous people? It's simple. I believe the officer is born with those traits. Rather than use them to hurt others, the officer chooses to use them for good.

The officers who hunt the wolves operate in a shadow world. A newly minted officer working with an undercover unit observing various drug deals in broad daylight as a part of their field training is surprised at what occurs in broad daylight, out in the open and unbeknownst to the civilians at a shopping plaza. The undercover officer responds, "stuff like this happens all the time."

A police officer, driving in a cruiser, patrols the streets of a city. The officer observes a subject that just doesn't fit in; the officer just has a gut feeling about this person. Something is off. The officer stops his cruiser and exits the vehicle. The subject sees the officer and runs. After a brief foot chase, the officer apprehends the subject with the assistance of fellow officers—and finds drugs and a loaded pistol on the person.

A policeman, while patrolling a neighborhood, recognizes the car of a suspect who has a warrant for his or her arrest. The officer notifies dispatch and coordinates the responding officers to surround the house. The officer and a few others meet with the suspect's relative outside the home. The officers, along with the relative, enter the home and look for the suspect. The relative is adamant that the suspect is not there. The officer is drawn, for some reason, to the bathroom. The officer opens the linen closet, observes a crawl space and sees the suspect's face. The officer apprehends the suspect.

In the worlds of drugs, human trafficking, child porn, terrorism, and gangs there are those that are always out there, keeping the public safe, working long hours, and putting their lives in danger. These types of cops are a rare breed. They are usually tatted up with beards and do not look like the typical uniformed cop. They are more than Sheepdogs. They are Hybrid Wolves. They are the last line of defense.

9

THE HYBRID WOLF
(PART 1)

"Let your plans be dark and impenetrable as night, and when you move,
fall like a thunderbolt."—Sun Tzu

There are Hybrid Wolves who work in the shadow world. They are rough looking, with tattoos, multiple rings on fingers, chains on their necks, baggy clothing, but there is a sense of code within them. They have a sense of honor, a sense of service to others. They work in professions that range from law enforcement to military special forces. They are cops, who work in specialty units such as gangs, narcotics, guns, federal task force, undercover, and SWAT. They are U.S. Army Special Forces, U.S. Marines MARSOC, U.S. Navy SEALs, U.S. Air Force PJs, etc. They walk out the door of their homes and leave their hearts with their loved ones. They enter a world of eat or be eaten, hunter or be hunted, predator or prey.

The other night, I had a dream, which inspired me to write about this topic. Living a life of duality can sometimes mix with your personal life. In this dream, I was going about being a cop. I was at some construction site in the city where I work. I heard a commotion nearby and saw a man with a large crowbar destroying a car. A woman on the other side of the car was screaming, "MY BABY, MY BABY!" She was panicking, trying to get her child out of a car seat. I ran toward them and drew my weapon.

I yelled to the man, "STOP, POLICE, DROP THE CROWBAR!" The man turned to me, eyes red with evil, he ran at me, full speed. I opened fire, 3 rounds center mass, he went down. Deep inside I was satisfied with the "kill", the Hybrid Wolf side was satisfied with the kill, with saving that woman and child, with protecting the citizens (pack) I am sworn to protect.

My dream quickly shifted to the next day, I felt hurt that I took a life. Hurt that I had to resort to violence to save another. Hurt that the man may have had a bad day and didn't intend to harm the woman and child but was taking out on an inanimate object. My dream shifted again. I was driving in my car, then suddenly I was in the woods, I was no longer in my car. I was running around, hunting, avoiding, my primal senses running wild. I finally woke up and thought: "What The Fuck?"

I rarely dream these days due to the medications I have been given by the VA. That's a blessing all on its own because when I did dream, it wasn't good, and I was up most nights. But that is a topic for another day. So, what the hell was that dream about? I did some self-analyzing.

This life of duality was represented in my dream. The "two sides" of me. The two different people I have to become. One of them is this Hybrid Wolf, the other is a father, husband, human. The Hybrid Wolf in me was born early in my life. He was born into war. As a 5-year-old kid living in war-torn Lebanon, I remember seeing artillery raining down on a mountainside near my village. I saw militia driving through the village, I was scared, I cried. Those were just a couple of incidents I've witnessed. Never mind the ones that I have probably suppressed.

This Hybrid Wolf, that was born early in my life became part of me. That part of me is what drives me, it's that little wind that stokes the fire inside me that turns into an inferno when needed.

The husband, father, human side of me is gentle, caring, tries to give all to my family. When my son asks me to play with him, whether it's wrestling, playing a video game, or even imagination play, I play with him. When my wife gives me a "honey-do" list, I go about doing them, and whatever else I am to do as a loving husband and father. Talk about two different lifestyles.

The dream represented the struggle I have daily with my human side and Hybrid Wolf side. We all have that in these professions. The hunter is not going to play with his children during the time of the hunt. A predator, as he stalks his prey, does not have the time or awareness to do a "honey-do" list. I am reminded daily that when I come home, the Hybrid Wolf stays outside the door. The human in me now takes over. Bills to pay, dad stuff, husband stuff, cleaning up, homework help, yard work, etc.

At times they clash. Here are a couple of examples. One day, I got home and got a phone call. This phone call was important since I was working undercover and the person on the other end was the target of an investigation. I picked up the line, walked into my house, dropping F-Bombs, "talking like a gangster," my tone was so different, my family didn't even recognize me since I was being a different person. My wife told me, "DON'T COME IN THE HOUSE TALKING LIKE THAT AGAIN." I had to chuckle because it was different, it was vulgar.

Another time, the SWAT team I'm on received a warning order of an upcoming operation. I spent the next few days working on the intel of the house and layout, preparing my gear, learning about the targets and encounters, my phone was constantly ringing with phone calls and text messages, etc. I was reprimanded a few days later. I was told I was not present in the house. Sure, I was there physically but my mind was somewhere else. I was in the "hunt" and removed all my other responsibilities. I have to be constantly reminded to leave my Hybrid Wolf at the door.

This dream I had, in the end, showed me my daily struggle I have. It showed me that there is a constant fight between my human side and primal side. Modern society has demonized and vilified that primal side. A modern-day warrior needs both the human and primal side to be successful. Not because they get satisfied with the kill but because of what happens after the kill. The human part reacts physiologically, emotionally, and spiritually. The human part preserves your humanity, so you don't lose it. One without the other is like a yin without the yang. It is the light versus the dark. In closing, there is a quote I'd like to share with you.

10

THE HYBRID WOLF (PART 2)

"Whoever fights monsters
should see to it that in the process
he does not become a monster.
And if you gaze long enough into an abyss,
the abyss will gaze back into you."
- Friedrich Nietzsche

I've been asked repeatedly to discuss my philosophy of the Hybrid Wolf. I'm going to expand on my previous article, "A Predator Hunting Predators" that I wrote for Havok Journal in June of 2020. Let me start by saying that Lieutenant Colonel Dave Grossman ignited a conversation within the law enforcement community about the sheepdog mentality. I agreed with most of what he has written about the topic. I feel there should be a further conversation about a type of police officer that is always overlooked: the Hybrid Wolf police officer.

Who are the police officers, military members, and others with a sheepdog mentality? LTC Grossman describes them as protecting the flock from the wolves by combining elements of both the sheep and the wolf. They are empathetic toward others, yet they understand violence and aggression. Most importantly, they know how to use their aggression to protect others.

Someone with a sheepdog mentality is not out roaming the streets looking for the wolves. If they are police officers, they respond to calls, protect others who need protection, and are tied to the radio. Proactive police work is not at the forefront. If an emergency arises, they run toward the sound of gunfire. They do what's necessary to save lives. People see them all the time, sitting at a traffic post, engaging with the community when told to do so, doing just enough to arrest if required.

Heraclitus once said, "Out of every one hundred men, ten shouldn't even be there, eighty are just targets, nine are the real fighters, and we are lucky to have them, for they make the battle. Ah, but the one, one is a warrior, and he will bring the others back." Now let's break this down even further. Let's use his quote in terms of a police department. In a police department of one hundred officers, I agree that ten shouldn't even be there. They are your sheep. They are just there to collect a paycheck and health insurance. They did not realize what they were getting into when signing the dotted line. The eighty that are just targets, yeah, we all know them. They are window-dressing. They look good in uniform, but their mindset is god-awful. I lump them with the ten sheep. Nine are real fighters, and they are your sheepdogs. They train, they know that danger lurks, they are proficient in their respective disciplines, and they are more than window-dressing.

Now the one, yes, the one is the Hybrid Wolf. That officer has truly embraced the primal instinct, the willingness to make the ultimate sacrifice so that others can go home. This officer puts the mission first. This officer is the hunter. This officer seeks out the wolf. This officer does not wait for the crisis to happen. This officer prevents the active shooter, the terrorist attack, the gang shootout, or the homicidal maniac hell-bent on killing.

This officer is in tune with the traits of a wolf. "If you wish to control others, you must control yourself," Miyamoto Musashi once said. The officer, who is the Hybrid Wolf, knows this very well. The officer has that predatory instinct under control. Jordan Peterson once said, "A harmless man is not a good man. A good man is a very dangerous man who has that danger under voluntary control."

Retired US Army Special Forces and Delta Force Operator Kyle Lamb told me a story of a police recruit training video. The recruiting video showed a cop face painting and playing with water balloons at the park. A second video showed a cop getting ready for a tour of duty. Strapping on the vest, loading the firearm, and getting ready for a shift. The police leadership did not like the second video. They felt it was a "little bit tough," whatever that means. Kyle asked, what kind of cop do you want on your police force? Do you want the cop who trains, who is proficient, who is ready to inflict violence on those who want to hurt, kill, and/or destroy our way of life? Or do you want a cop who does face painting but does not understand the other part of the job? The real police work. Where the officer has to be out there, constantly scanning, hunting for the wolf. The part that counts.

One thing I want to make absolutely clear Hybrid Wolf cops, military members, are not out-of-control individuals. In fact, they are in complete control of their instincts and are able to channel the wolf side for the betterment of society. They are not the kinds of cops who end up on the evening news because of charges of excessive force. They mock those officers who engage in such behavior because they knew they didn't have any control from the start.

A Hybrid Wolf officer understands that aggression is a gift. It is a survival instinct that must be embraced and trained for. The wolf, when it strikes, strikes with intensity and ferocity. Most police officers do not know what to do with that type of aggression. A Hybrid Wolf knows that aggression and responds in kind.

When cop killers are interviewed in prison and are asked why they killed the police officers, most of their answers are because they knew they could. I know cops across the country, who are Hybrid Wolves, and they tell me all the time that there is only one reason some of their fellow officers weren't killed in certain situations. It's because the bad guy decided not to.

The Hybrid Wolf cop, military member, firefighter, and any other warrior, represent a very small population. They are out there but not seen. This is because they prefer to operate in the shadows. They get frustrated by their fellow warriors who do not get their mentality. They are out there hunting, combing the world for the beast that they know is out there. It's a beast they understand because, at one point, they recognized the beast in themselves and decided to keep it under voluntary control.

11

THE OATH: A WARRIOR'S CORE BELIEF

"Loyalty to country ALWAYS. Loyalty to government, when it deserves it."— Mark Twain

When you listen to the National Anthem, do you get tingles that run up your spine? When you see someone in need, do you help? Is there something deep in your core? For us, who raised our right hand and swore the oath, we believe in the oath, and that it is worth dying for:

"I, (state your name), do solemnly swear
that I will support and defend the Constitution of the United States
against all enemies, foreign and domestic;
that I will bear true faith and allegiance to the same;
and that I will obey the orders of the President of the United States
and the orders of the officers appointed over me,

according to regulations and the Uniform Code of Military Justice. So help
me God."

I remember making that oath. I remember heading off to boot camp, and the pride I felt when I graduated. That oath represented who I was, not just as an American but as a human being. Some people are born with a moral compass. Most need religion or a law to teach them right from wrong. There is a popular Spartan story, and it goes like this:

An old man was looking for a seat at the Olympic games. The crowd was clearly annoyed by the old man until a Spartan offered his seat. The crowd applauded and the old man turned to them and said "All Greeks know what is right, but only Spartans do it."

The above story illustrates my point. Some are born with a moral compass to do what is right. Others may know the right thing to do but will not do it. How many times have you seen "viral" videos of people in distress? It never ceases to amaze me, in this modern time, what people will do to get their five minutes of fame.

As a cop, I made a similar oath, nearly the same one as I did in the military. Below is an example of an oath a Law Enforcement officer takes.

Law Enforcement Oath of Honor
On my honor, I will never
betray my badge, my integrity,
my character or the public trust.
I will always have the courage to hold
myself and others accountable for our actions.
I will always uphold the constitution,
my community and the agency I serve.

When swearing an oath, it's not just an oath to the country but also to your fellow man. It is an oath sworn to your brothers and sisters in the service; an oath sworn to your brothers and sisters in law enforcement.

Those of us who take this oath to heart acknowledge that it never expires as long as we live. Even off duty, some of us see things, notice things out of the ordinary. There are some in the profession who once told me, "I'M NOT REQUIRED TO ACT." I couldn't believe what I heard. I responded, "YOU'RE A COP." We argued for a little while and I realized that some people are just there to collect a check and work overtime. This is a very small percentage of cops in the business, but it is sad that this behavior is allowed. It forced me to question the oath that this officer made. It tells me that they don't believe in it.

Our oath is part of our core beliefs. It is a part of who we are. You see them every day. How many videos are out there showing off-duty cops, firemen, veterans, active-duty soldiers, Marines, and others springing into action without any hesitation. They are among the best in our society because of what their core beliefs are. It's not just an oath to them. It is a way of life.

12

THE FACE OF BURDEN

Why are you always intense?

Why are you always mean?

Why are you always angry?

You look like you've been through hell.

These are just some of the questions and statements civilians have commented to me.

When someone looks at my face, the intensity is obvious. But what is unknown is the SWAT operation I just took part in to capture a dangerous child sex predator. What is unknown is how I nearly pulled the trigger because the predator decided to reach for a Glock 9mm sitting on his bed as I made entry. He then stopped suddenly and raised his hands.

When someone looks at my face the meanness is apparent. What is unknowable is that I what I've seen and felt are the realities of the world that I've shouldered for decades, the years of experiencing one tragedy after another, and which are now visible on my face and can no longer be hidden.

My innocence was stripped from me when I went to war as a young adult. A part of me has never left that fight. A part of me will always be there. As a cop, I have witnessed car crashes, stabbings, homicides, shooting victims, children who have been sexually abused, and a failing system that doesn't work the way it should because of stakeholders who don't allow it to work.

I have performed CPR in an attempt to save a life only to have that life get taken away.

When someone looks at my face the anger is visible. What is not obvious is the emotional weight I take on when watching children get taken from their homes. Anger is there because of the failed parents I run into day in and day out. They use their children as leverage. They abuse their children. I know removing the children is for the best, but the feeling is still there. More anger comes from having to tell parents their addicted child is now dead. The young die too soon.

When people say to me, "You look like you've been through hell," what no one knows is that I carry with me every call, every scream, every explosion, every SWAT callout, and every mission at war. I "look like I've been through hell" from years of navigating the tragedies of the world so my country doesn't have to.

My core beliefs of honor, self-less service, integrity, courage, and discipline are more than just words. They are part of the shield I carry to protect the innocents from the horrors buried deep in my face.

For the combat veterans and police officers, my face of burden is a gift to my country. Civilians cannot fathom this weight. This face is my love for humanity, this face doesn't smile easily because of what tomorrow may bring.

13

THE DEATH OF THE MODERN DAY WARRIOR

"Nobody Loves a Warrior Until the Enemy Is at the Gate"—*Unknown*

There is such a massive disconnect between the warrior class and the civilian class in the modern world. Yes, I did say warrior class. I do believe that there is a warrior class. The warrior class is a small group of the modern population. They are service members, first responders, and members of certain other professions.

In ancient times, thousands of years ago, warriors were looked at as the protectors of their lands, homes, country. They were revered, loved, feared, and respected. They had a strict code to abide by. They were disciplined in their skillset. They studied warfare, and it was a part of their lives. It was a way of life.

In modern times, some civilian leaders seem to be disconnected from their first responders and military. They do not understand a warrior's mindset, so they try to get rid of the class altogether. Some police academies no longer induce stress on recruits, military leadership courses do not challenge future leaders enough, the new generation of warriors are becoming fewer and fewer due to participation trophies, social media, and game consoles. Since this has been happening, some police officers that graduate these "stress-free" academies are already being set up to fail. They do not know how they are going to react under real stress. It's the same with soldiers graduating boot camp and eventually going to war. They also do not know how to respond to stress. If the officer, soldier, firefighter, or EMT does not know how to respond under stress, it is a recipe for disaster. Sometimes mistakes and even fatal mistakes are made.

True modern-day warriors understand the risks and continually push their limits. It's a discipline and a way of life. In the law enforcement community, unfortunately for some, it is not a way of life. Some officers want to go in, work a road detail, collect their overtime, and do the bare minimum on their shift. They do not have a warrior code. I have seen some officers go the long way to a fight in progress call, I have seen some officers avoid confrontation at all costs. Not because they are doing a good job in diffusing a situation but because they are not confident in their abilities. This is dangerous. It causes modern-day warriors not to trust their fellow officers to back them up.

A few years ago, I was working my usual patrol sector. It was early Sunday morning and I observed two individuals in a city-owned park. Typically, we find out that people are selling drugs, doing drugs, drinking alcohol, and a whole myriad of situations. I went in to investigate. I discovered a man and a woman. The woman was extremely nervous, so that set off some red flags in my head. I interviewed both of them and let dispatch know what I had observed. At this point the usual procedure is that your beat partner would arrive to back you up. That morning my beat partner was nowhere to be seen.. Later, I got a phone call from the shift commander and was asked where my beat partner was. I said I didn't know. A fellow warrior would not do that. A modern-day warrior would never leave a colleague to deal with a potential volatile situation.

It turned out that the woman was having an affair with the man.

"The greatest counterpoise to fear, the ancients believed, is love—the love of the individual warrior for his brothers in arms. At Thermopylae on the final morning, when the last surviving Spartans knew they were all going to die, they turned to one of their leaders, the platoon commander Dienekes, and asked him what thoughts they should hold in their minds in this final hour to keep their courage strong. Dienekes instructed his comrades to fight not in the name of such lofty concepts as patriotism, honor, duty or glory. Don't even fight, he said, to protect your family or your home. The soldier's prayer today on the eve of battle remains not "Lord, spare me," but "Lord, let me not prove unworthy of my brothers."-Steven Pressfield: The Warrior Ethos.

Talk to any combat veteran, any police officer who had to run into a gunfight, any firefighter who had to run into a burning building, and they will tell you the same thing. They were more concerned about failing their fellow man, their partners, their fellow warriors than for their personal safety. It is something ingrained in their DNA. Unfortunately, modern-day society is causing that part of the DNA to deactivate. It is done through ad campaigns, activists, political leaders, and others who do not understand warrior culture. They demonize the profession.

Political agendas, election season, social media, traditional media, the list goes on. Those groups and agendas are slowly killing off the concept of modern-day warriors. They are now demonized and are the "bad guys." And all because of an extremely small group of bad ones.

The United States is headed down a dangerous road. Without modern-day warriors, who will protect the people? Who will step up when the citizens need them? Yeah, I know, the keyboard rangers out there will say "oh that's why we have the second amendment" or "I can do blah blah blah..." Let's come back to the real world. Most people do not have it in them to do that kind of work. When the shots are fired, an exceedingly small number of people will run toward the gunfire. Being warriors is an honor, all of them should hold their heads high. Warriors need to be understood and accepted as they are. They man the walls, they stand the watch, they are ready to fight the enemies, wherever they may come from.

14

ARE YOU A BOSS OR A LEADER

"Leadership is not about being in charge. Leadership is about taking care of those in your charge."—Simon Sinek

There are many seminars, speakers and classes concerning leadership: how to lead and how to supervise. There are a ton of books out there regarding these very topics. People pay hundreds of dollars to listen to someone tell them how to lead. I am not a supervisor at work, but I will provide a lens into why I differentiate between bosses and leaders. Is there really a difference between the leader and a boss?

A boss is someone in a leadership position such as shift supervisor, manager, vice president, police leader or military leader. A boss is one who demands, one who rules with an authoritarian hand, one who repeatedly reminds the staff of rank. I have dealt with bosses throughout my life. They were managers, police leaders, or military leaders. I've come to realize they all have similar traits. These traits include micro-managing, lacking trust, showing little or no concern for the welfare or their workers, accusing too quickly, providing no clear expectations, and reminding everyone "who's the boss".

A leader is someone who can motivate others toward a common goal. The leader has strong interpersonal skills, a strong personality, and the ability to use the strengths evident in others. A leader is in the trenches rather than sitting comfortably in an office.

At the start of my law enforcement career, I was working New Year's Eve. It was cold, the wind was biting, and most of the officers were outside in the city. Most of us were either wearing winter caps or watch caps to keep our heads warm. A deputy chief drove around and ordered all of us to wear our regular hats because he did not like the look of the winter caps. Meanwhile, he drove around in a nice, warm police car. That pissed a lot of us off. As soon as he left, we all went back to wearing our winter caps.

Here is an example of great police leadership: I received a phone call at 1 am from my police department stating there was a drive-by shooting in the city and all detectives were being called in. We investigated the shooting for over 20 hours straight. We caught all those involved. Our unit commander gave me and my partner the rest of the evening shift off so we could go home and sleep. As soon as my head hit the pillow, I was asleep.

Here is an example of poor military leadership: We were all at the range one day. a lieutenant colonel, probably the most miserable asshole I've ever met, was in charge of the Battalion at the time. He yelled at this private he caught sleeping in the bleachers. A few minutes later, we found the lieutenant colonel asleep in a separate part of the bleachers. Pictures were taken of him for laughs. He was not respected at all. He was a horrible "leader." He was definitely a "boss".

Here's an example of great military leadership. In my squad in Iraq, we were the Battalion Commander's (BN CMDR) Personal Security Detail (PSD). The BN CMDR was one busy leader. Our BN covered a large area of operation (AO). So, we would travel far and wide to check on every unit under his command. Our furthest drive took over 15 hours through insurgent, terrorist and IED infested roads. The BN CMDR would also have us patrol our AO. He was always right there with us. Day or night. Sleep or no sleep. He was out there with us. If got to a large base that had a cafeteria, he would have us go eat first and he would stay with our gun trucks. He taught me a lot about what being a good leader was all about. He did not merely supervise; he led.

I have met spectacular leaders. Some of these leaders didn't have any rank. They were not supervisors or managers. Sometimes leaders are already within an organization and do not need rank to have people follow them. Leaders know how to take control of a situation and adapt to whatever working conditions are presented to them. They inspire others to follow suit. Sometimes, it's unbeknownst to the leader him or herself that they have had that effect on others.

A leader leads, a boss supervises. Let's think about this for a second. In the Army we have a saying, "lead from the front," a phrase used a lot by officers and non-commissioned officers alike. A leader works with the team until the mission is done. A leader is first to arrive and last to leave. A leader spends time getting to know his or her people. A leader cleans up with their team. A leader eats last. A leader acknowledges the successes of the team and not his or hers. A leader scolds in private and praises in public. A boss sits back and gives the people work to do. A boss supervises and micromanages. A boss takes credit for the work that the team has done. A boss scolds in public and hardly ever praises. A boss works the team to the point of exhaustion. A boss does not know his or her team very well.

Are you a boss? Or are you a leader? Why?

THE DARK

Amongst you, I walk
Quiet, Alone, and full of rage,
Echoes of battles ringing in my ears.

The demons I came home with I locked them in a cage,
Afraid of what can happen If they break out and play.

At night I lay in bed,
My head feels like it is splitting in two,
Each hemisphere of my brain
Pulling to unravel the dark inside.
I wake up with sharp pain in the back of my head.

A voice says to me
Come back,
Come back to the fight.
A part of me never left,
A part of me is still fighting,
A part of me is forever in the dark.

The dark in me,
Forever in me.

15

I'M NOT LIBERAL, I AM NOT CONSERVATIVE, I AM REASONABLE

These days in America, if you have an opinion (no matter what that opinion may be), you are quickly labeled and ridiculed. It could be the most well-thought-out answer to a question. There is so much "noise", it has drowned out the most important trait out there. It has many names, but I'll just go with 'reasonable'. There are so many social media platforms that lump you into a group. You will be labeled as a liberal or a conservative. I have a problem with that, as most of you should.

A couple of years ago, I recall Facebook labeling political affiliations based on someone's online activity. I remember checking it and I was labeled, "ultra-conservative." I laughed at that. My online activity involves a lot of research, writing, music, and various other subjects. I surmised that because I'm a cop and a combat veteran, I'm identified as an ultra-conservative. In addition, I read all kinds of news, and posts, as well as follow a wide spectrum of journalists, U.S. Supreme Court rulings, and various government entities because I like to be well-informed.

I'll ask you: Does that make me an ultra-conservative? Since when is being informed equated to being a radical? I ask this of both sides. How about instead of that label, we go with "reasonable."

That's all I am: reasonable.

Hot button topics have plagued our newsfeeds. The dopamine dump of confirmation bias has become exponentially worse. A meme with false information becomes the talk of the internet and most people just fall right in line. Here's an example: I was watching a YouTube video featuring Aziz Ansari. He's a comedian if you don't know who he is, and he was talking about the media. During a show, he asked the audience for their thoughts on the customer who complained to Pizza Hut management after finding pepperoni arranged as a swastika on his pizza. Aziz tells the audience to clap if they saw the picture.

Some did. Aziz then says to the audience to clap if they thought this person was just looking for attention; again people clapped. He went as far as asking someone in the audience if he had seen the picture and he said that he did. He also said he thought the customer was looking for attention. Aziz revealed to the audience that he made up that whole story and it never even happened.

The point he wanted to make was to show how gullible people are to believe anything they read or even think that they read or saw. People are no longer reasonable. They will just go with whatever is the hot-button topic. As Aziz says, people are trying to "out-woke" each other. It was very simple for him to trick them.

As a cop, I research a lot of different things, I like to be well-informed. I have read about different hate groups, communist groups, Black Lives Matter, ISIS, and different books about different ideologies. If you search my history, it's going to be full of things like that. Does reading or researching any of these things make me a liberal or a conservative? NO. It helps me understand the why. That's what most have lost today, the ability to ask why. People no longer listen; they just talk over each other. The loudest and most obnoxious one wins.

I recently listened to DC lawmakers question Joint-Chiefs Chairman General Mark Milley regarding a "woke" military, and I believe he said it best. "I want to understand white rage, and I'm white. What is it that caused thousands of people to assault this building and try to overturn the Constitution of the United States of America? I've read Mao Tse Tung. I've read Karl Marx. I've read Lenin. That doesn't make me a communist. So, what is wrong with understanding, having some situational understanding, about the country for which we are here to defend?"

The past few years, when President Trump was in office, I'd keep getting asked, "Are you a Trump supporter?" or "Are you a Biden supporter?" My answer has always been the same.

I'm for whoever does right by the American people, veterans, and our Nation. That's it. Does that make me left or right, liberal or conservative?

No.

I have very close friends, brothers-in-arms, and we discuss various issues. If we don't agree, I don't cut them off and refuse to be friends anymore. Just because they have a different point of view doesn't mean I can't be their friend. It does not matter to me. If you have an argument or a point of view, make sure you give me facts before your opinion. I mean, isn't that what critical thinking is?

I am not a conservative or a liberal, I am just a guy who has a point of view on many different social topics. I research, I read, I listen and then I form my own decision based on all the facts. A lot of Americans do not do that anymore because it's so much easier to be told what to believe versus seeking the truth out. That's what made America great. It's the thirst for knowledge.

My family's home country in Lebanon is thousands of years old, and in America, we made it to the moon. A 300-year-old country beat the rest of the world on many things. Why? Because of our thirst for knowledge. Let's bring that back, let's start asking the hard questions, and let's seek out truth versus being told what is true.

16

POLITICIANS ARE THE NEW RADICAL EXTREMISTS

"There is nothing noble in being superior to your fellow man; true nobility is being superior to your former self."— *Ernest Hemingway*

I was born in 1981 in a conflict zone in Monrovia, Liberia. My parents fled with my brother and me to Lebanon. Lebanon wasn't any better. I have seen extremism in the three major religions all my life. We ended up finding peace in America. A peace that a majority in the U.S. takes for granted. Over the years growing up in America, I witnessed how it slowly changed. Not for the better, but for the worse. Now we are faced with a different form of extremism: Political Extremism.

I was born into war and bred into conflict zones. I have memories of soldiers getting blown up and artillery raining down on a mountainside. I remember running to my mother, crying hysterically, because some sort of militia came into our village in Lebanon. I joined the U.S. Army after 9/11 and went to war for our country. I wanted to show that not all people from the Middle East are radical Muslims. The extremists in the community told me I joined the enemy. In reality, I wanted to root out the evil that plagued the land, that these intellectual imams are the extremists, and use religion to mask their true desires.

How bad is extremism? Well for example, in Lebanon, Al Qaeda terrorists had spoons in their pockets because they were led to believe that if they died during combat they would dine with the Prophet. Now, this is just religion being extreme. How does it tie into politics?

The common theme I hear now in politics is fear-based. On both sides of the aisle. All of a sudden, politicians are the new priests, and what they say is considered fact. People have stopped questioning politicians' motives behind any claim they spout.

After 9/11, people looked to their elected leaders for some sort of closure, guidance, and resolve. The political war machine was fueled by the anger of the American public, and rightfully so. When Japan bombed Pearl Harbor, Naval Marshal General Isoroku Yamamoto said, "I fear all we have done is to awaken a sleeping giant and fill him with a terrible resolve." I believe the same thing happened after 9/11. The American people, no matter what color, creed, or religion, wanted one thing: justice.

Now let's fast forward to current times in the United States. For the past decade or more, politicians have created a fear-based campaign. "THEY ARE GOING TO TAKE OUR GUNS." Guns fly off the shelves and people stack up on ammo. That is the most common phrase that I hear from one side of the aisle. "POLICE MURDER ALL BLACK MEN." Is that from the other side now? The people are bombarded with "statistics" and so-called "experts" on the media that fan the flames for the political extremists.

It is no different from when I was at war. I remember sitting in a courtyard outside of our barracks in Mosul. I was listening to the evening prayers at a local mosque down the street. I remember the Shiekh, or Imam, speaking to the worshipers. He kept referring to the evil that has plagued the land, meaning U.S. forces and those that conspire with American forces, and that they need to banish this evil in the name of God at whatever cost. It was their duty as Muslims. The conspirators he was talking about were interpreters and those who aided U.S. Forces to combat the radicals. This is a so-called intelligent religious figure preaching to his followers and exhorting them to bring about the death of those who are different.

Political extremism is just as dangerous as religious extremism. They both feed fear to the people. They both use extreme measures to get their point of view out there. Just because religious extremism is more direct doesn't mean that political extremism isn't as dangerous. Political extremism took years to infiltrate society. It took time, strategy, and placing the right political figures in the right spots. Look at what we have now. Look at our so-called ELECTED leaders. They have caused this division, not the people. I have seen this in the past. I have seen this growing up in war-torn countries and I have seen it while at war.

It is now here at our home.

17

LAW ENFORCER VS. CONSTITUTIONAL PROTECTOR: WE NEED BOTH

"People sleep peaceably in their beds at night only because rough men stand ready to do violence on their behalf."— George Orwell

I've mentioned numerous times the idea of two different kinds of cops. There is the Sheepdog and there is the Hybrid Wolf. But let's go even deeper. Let's get closer to their core; to their morals, ideals, whatever you might call it. Let's dig into their minds.

Some cops just enforce the law. You speed, you get a fine. You have a broken taillight; you get a ticket. You run a stop sign; the officer gives you a fine. You "jaywalk", the officer gives you a fine. The officer is merely following the letter of the law. What does the letter of the law mean? The letter of the law can be any formal code, rule, regulation, policy, or principle that must be followed according to the government.

In simple terms, it's the law. Letters of the law range from traffic laws to crimes against people and property. All these laws are in place to serve, maintain, and protect the public welfare in various ways. One true thing, not all these laws are popular among police officers, but to law enforcers, they choose to follow the letter of the law as it is stated. Nothing more, nothing less, and nothing personal to the public.

I've known many cops who are like that. They are a great group of guys and gals, but I believe they fit that mold of being a Sheepdog. They respond when called and will do what needs to be done to the letter of the law. In the profession, we do crack jokes about the law enforcers by saying things like, "OH YOU'LL GIVE A TICKET TO SOMEONE WHO FORGOT TO GET AN INSPECTION STICKER BUT NEVER MIND THE DEAD PERSON IN THE BACK SEAT OF THE CAR." It's dark humor but you get the point.

There are officers out there that are Constitutional Protectors, who follow the spirit of the law. Officers who follow the spirit of the law are more sympathetic to the public and truly believe in serving the public, more than enforcing certain laws. These officers are not concerned about someone jaywalking. These officers are hunters of evil. They are more concerned with murder, sexual predators, truly evil people who prey on the weak. They have been this way since they were children. These types do not need a law or a commandment to tell them, "Thou shall not kill." They were already born with a moral compass. They stood up to bullies as kids, they protected their friends and strangers alike. They stop to help a motorist in need.

I am going to share a story of a situation I was involved in. A few years ago, I was on uniformed patrol in my sector. I received a call regarding a shoplifting incident that occurred at a Stop and Shop. I walked into the establishment, and the loss prevention officer met with me and provided me with evidence: footage, a license plate number, and some of the items that were stolen. From what I could tell, it was all food items. I tracked down the suspect and went to their home. I knocked at the door and spoke with a family member. I learned the food was stolen for their family. The primary caretaker had been out of work for some time and had not been able to find another job. The fridge was empty, the family needed food. I felt bad for this family. All I could think of was this could happen to me. I ended up letting the family keep the food. Now, these types of stories happen all the time across the U.S. But no one hears about them because they are not newsworthy.

Across the country, during the COVID-19 pandemic, numerous states wanted law enforcement to issue fines to individuals who crossed state lines. This order was a direct threat to the constitutionally protected freedom of movement. Bloomberg Law did an article on this on August 2nd, 2020.

In Rhode Island, Gov. Gina Raimondo (D) invoked public health emergency powers to order State Police to stop any car with New York license plates, and National Guard troops to go door-to-door to find people who have traveled recently from New York, ordering them to self-quarantine or face jail time or fines.

In Florida, Gov. Ron DeSantis (R) issued a mandatory 14-day quarantine of any traveler from New York, New Jersey, and Connecticut.

Kansas, Hawaii, South Carolina, and Alaska have done the same as Florida. Counties in North Carolina and Wisconsin turned around people in vehicles with out-of-state plates seeking access to resort properties they owned.

On March 28, 2020, President Donald Trump said that he would order a federal quarantine of people from the New York tri-state area. New York Gov. Andrew Cuomo (D) responded with a threat to sue; and coronavirus task force members persuaded the president to instead issue a travel advisory.

"While the powers of governors and the president in a public health emergency are extensive, these measures to halt travel inside the U.S. tore at the underpinnings of our federalist system which divides power between the federal government and the states."

The above is an exact quote from the Bloomberg article. A cop, who is a law enforcer, would enforce whatever the governor orders. A cop, who is a constitutional protector, would not enforce such an order. The order violates his or her moral compass, belief in The Constitution, and the constitutionally protected freedom of movement.

Are all police officers the same? No. Every encounter a person has with a police officer will be different. Each officer is either a law enforcer (Sheepdog) or a constitutional protector (Hybrid Wolf). Each officer handles situations differently. The law enforcer has a place in society and so does the constitutional protector. Both play a role in serving and protecting the public they serve.

18

EVERYONE LOSES WHEN WE MAKE POLICE SCAPEGOATS FOR BAD POLICIES

"People will do anything, no matter how absurd, to avoid facing their own souls."— Carl Gustav Jung

It was a beautiful day. Kids were running around, dogs were playing, and hot dogs and burgers were on the grill. My son was laughing it up with his friends. We were at a birthday party for one of his classmates. I was talking to a group of parents. I didn't really know them. I tend to be cautious about revealing whether or not I'm a cop and rely on my "Spidey" senses to let me know when to do so.

Sometimes my wife and son tell people. I always remind them of the dangers of telling the wrong person. But this venue was different. My instincts did not detect any danger. Everyone was pleasant and helpful about keeping an eye on all the kids. One of the parents asked me, "What do you do for work?"

I responded with, "I work for the city's Department of Public Works (DPW)." Why did I just say that? Why did I lie when I did not feel any danger? I thought about it long and hard for the rest of the day and realized...the badge has been tarnished and shamed. It's no longer a prestigious job. Honor is no longer associated with it.

I graduated from the police academy in 2007. My academy class was in formation outside and we were getting ready to swear our oaths. A ton of civilians were watching, cheering, clapping. The badge was shiny and the badge had honor. It was a great feeling. From the moment I stepped into my uniform to when I was assigned a cruiser and got my first call, I was a police officer.

I was who people turned to for help. I prevented crimes from occurring, I settled disputes, I summonsed or arrested criminals. I have seen pure evil and have seen victims of circumstance. Besides war, the faces of the dead and murdered, stay with me. I suspect a majority of police officers reading this are nodding their heads in agreement.

Being a cop, in this day in age in the United States, has been vilified. Vilified by the very politicians who made these awful policies and laws that the police are required to enforce. An article, written by a former mayor of Minneapolis, Betsy Hodges, truly highlighted the disconnect between law enforcement officers and politicians:

"I remember clearly one officer, a middle-aged white man, who is now a sergeant with the department, looking me dead in the eye and cursing me out in front of the entire room. I needed to take a walk in their shoes, he said, peppering his insults with profanity, so that I could 'know what that's like" He complained of protesters' 'calling us names, getting in our faces' and throwing objects at officers. And 'you're letting them,' he said.

"The not fully said bottom line of his message was clear: White liberals like me ask the police to do our dirty work — dealing with the racial and economic inequities our policies create. Normally, we turn a blind eye to the harsh methods that many of them use to achieve our goal of order, pretend that isn't what we've done, and then act surprised when their tough-guy behavior goes viral and gets renewed scrutiny.

"Whatever else you want to say about police officers, they know — whether they articulate it neatly or not — that we are asking them to step into a breach left by our bad policies. The creation of more-just systems won't guarantee the prevention of atrocities. But the status quo in cities, created by white liberals, invites brutal policing. "As Mayor of Minneapolis, I Saw How White Liberals Block Change" - The New York Times

Her statement said it all. Policies created by politicians put the police in a bad spot. Over a decade of these types of policies have tarnished the badge. Budget cuts, lack of proper training, lack of proper accountability, and the rapidly dropping hiring standards have placed individuals who shouldn't be cops on the job. These things caused the badge to become an object of shame.

It is a shame because the badge now reflects what American society has become. It is a shame that officers now are so demoralized that the truly evil are out there using this climate to their advantage. It is a shame that proactive officers are forced to sit back and watch society destroy itself from within. Now officers have to decide, whether an action is going to put them in jail, cause them to lose their home, or lose their family.

I have seen time and time again when officers would be justified in using force elect not to and get either seriously hurt or killed. I'm not saying let the bad ones get away with crimes, what I am saying is that the broad stroke of the media, politicians, and other groups has caused violence against good hardworking police officers. When you have a political figure, like Bernie Sanders, in a room full of college students, make an inflammatory statement like "if you disrespect a cop you will be shot in the back of the head." If you don't believe me, go on YouTube yourselves and look it up.

I speak to police officers across the country and the tone is the same. They are demoralized, beaten down, assaulted, and accused of being "murderers." Doesn't this sound familiar to events that occurred during the Vietnam War? I've written an article about the similarity between the treatment of police officers that is eerily like the way

Vietnam veterans were treated. The badge now represents shame. It is unfortunate and disturbing.

Society has picked its new scapegoat for the failure of policy and that is going to hurt us all in the end.

19

COPS FILL THE BREACH LEFT BY OUR BAD POLICIES

A Tale of Two Pictures.
Photo credit: Wikicommons

What is the difference between the two pictures above? They are in different eras of American history. One depicts protestors during the Vietnam War and the other is a protester in NYC. They both depict the failures of elected officials in Congress. They both depict the tension that has been building internally in America for decades. They both depict what it looks like when politicians no longer work for the people. What is happening right now in America with law enforcement resembles how the media and people treated Vietnam veterans when they returned home.

During an episode on *The Weekly Havok*, the host Chris Paul Meyer made a statement that got me thinking. He said, and I'm summarizing, police officers are being treated as Vietnam veterans were treated during and after the Vietnam War. Think about that statement. Both are victims of a failure in policy. The difference? They wear uniforms. They are out in public. Instead, most politicians pick and choose when they want to engage with the public.

I landed in the U.S. for my two weeks of leave from war back in 2005. I remember standing there at the passenger pick-up area of the airport waiting for a cab. I was in my Desert Camouflage Uniform (DCU). This woman, older, smug, looked at me and scoffed. She said, "baby killer." At the time, I was too tired to even give a shit what she said. This is minor compared to what Vietnam veterans endured. For the most part, the Global War on Terrorism veterans are truly loved and hailed as heroes. Vietnam War veterans were spat on, called names, etc. There were protests and riots...does this all sound familiar?

The media, certain politicians, and other groups painted a broad picture of the Vietnam War, just like the broad picture that has been painted of law enforcement in America. There is a saying, if you tell a lie long enough it becomes the truth. In this case, cops are racist, cops are bigots, cops target only people of color, cops kill only people of color and the list goes on.

Let's look at how Vietnam veterans are being treated now. The public has realized that the veterans were only doing their jobs. The public shifted their focus to the politicians of the time and the failed policies that were put in place.

Let's fast forward to today.

Certain policies and laws created by politicians put the police in a situation where instead of building community relationships, they are forced to be the hammer rather than true peace officers. During the justice department investigation into the Ferguson, Missouri, Police Department, "City officials have consistently set maximizing revenue as the priority for Ferguson's law enforcement activity...City and police leadership pressure officers to write citations, independent of any public safety need, and rely on citation productivity to fund the City budget."

In an email from March 2010, the Ferguson Finance Director wrote to Chief Jackson that "unless ticket writing ramps up significantly before the end of the year, it will be hard to significantly raise collections next year. What are your thoughts? Given that we are looking at a substantial sales tax shortfall, it's not an insignificant issue." Chief Jackson responded that the city would see an increase in fines when more officers were hired and that he could target the $1.5 million forecast.

Significantly, Chief Jackson stated that he was also "looking at different shift schedules which will place more officers on the street, which in turn will increase traffic enforcement per shift." This was a clear example of how city officials failed their citizens in every sense of the word. Using police to generate revenue for the city is the absolute worst method of policing. Police officers are not there to generate revenue for the city, they are there to foster community partnerships, protect and preserve life, charge individuals criminally when appropriate, and the list goes on.

So, when a major incident occurs because of poor policies, politicians quickly point their finger at who? The police, the military, whoever they decide is the scapegoat. Let's be frank for a minute. On a national level, statistics show that 120 negative police videos are posted in a year. In one year though, it is estimated that there are approximately 900 million police contacts. The true percentage of the negativity is .000013 percent. Let that soak in.

These days a cop must deal with a multitude of problems in our society. Most of it has to do with a failed mental health industry, especially after the COVID pandemic. I have personally seen the breakdown of the mental health system. We are dealing with far more emotionally disturbed persons (EDP) than before. In the city I where work, I had to involuntary commit three EDPs to the local hospital in one day. I have never done that before in my career. I have friends, who are cops, talking people off rooftops. Police have to wear multiple hats when they get to their calls. They have to be a social worker or a police officer in less than a second and be able to decide that split second.

I have said it before and I'll say it again, the anger and hate toward law enforcement is the sign of a society falling apart. When an officer goes to get coffee, the officer is hyper vigilant. The officer worries if the server is going to spit in their coffee or food. Law enforcement officers today are getting treated like Vietnam veterans in the 60s. The police have become the enemy of the people. Politicians use officers as scapegoats for their failed laws and policies.

The public takes it out on the police because they are the face of the government. They are the ones out there on the streets. Maybe one day the public will realize it. But by then, we may be left with very few good cops and have only those who just want a check at the end of the day and couldn't care less about the community.

20

WHY YOU WANT COPS TO HAVE A WARRIOR'S MINDSET

"When a warrior fights not for himself, but for his brothers, when his most passionately sought goal is neither glory nor his own life's preservation, but to spend his substance for them, his comrades, not to abandon them, not to prove unworthy of them, then his heart truly has achieved contempt for death, and with that he transcends himself and his actions touch the sublime."—Steven Pressfield

Over the last several years, the term "warrior" has been used, labeled, demonized, idolized, and applied to all kinds of professions. These days when someone mentions the word "warrior," typically it is synonymous with members of the military, sports figures, MMA, UFC, and others. The term "warrior" in the law enforcement community has been a taboo title. It was removed from culture and replaced with words like "guardian" and "sheepdog."

In the law enforcement community, when the word "warrior" was used, it was referred to as a mindset. The warrior mindset. Political correctness demonized it and associated it with part of the "militarization" of police. Across the country, that word was wiped out of any curriculum at police academies. It meant that police officers were too aggressive for modern society, it meant police officers were prone to use lethal force, it meant police officers would think of themselves as above their fellow man.

The warrior mindset is far from that. The core beliefs of someone adopting the warrior mindset are discipline, respect, selfless service, honor, courage, and integrity. A warrior mindset, at a deeper level, helps individuals realize the true enemy is not external forces but the internal. Weakness, fear, jealousy, greed, ego, laziness, and many other negative traits are recognized as the enemy of the warrior mindset. Miyamoto Musashi once said, "If you wish to control others you must control yourself." Think about it. Musashi did not mean to literally "control" people, he was referring to the idea of the "self." To have a warrior mindset is to look inward and defeat those negative traits in our hearts in order to be an effective officer in the community.

I placed fear in the above list of the negative traits. Let me clarify something: to be afraid is only natural. The greatest instinct in any animal, including humans, is self-preservation. Fear of death is an overwhelmingly powerful instinct that causes an enormous amount of panic. To have a warrior mindset means to fight against that fear for the betterment of your fellow man. The warrior fights that impulse to run away from an active shooter, a terrorist, a mass murderer, etc.

A person with a warrior mindset has two extremely powerful traits: honor and love; honor in their profession and love for their fellow man. To have honor in your profession means you dedicate your life to it. Let's be realistic for a moment. Whether being a member of the military or a first responder, it is a way of life. These professions are not a job, they are a way of life. Military members who dedicate their lives to the profession demonstrate this in the way they behave, expressed in the way they shoot, fight, and care for their comrades.

Leaders who have the warrior mindset are some of the best and strongest leaders in the military. The same goes for first responders.

A police officer who looks sharp, acts sharp, and takes the profession seriously is an officer I want responding to emergencies, not because he or she "looks good" in a uniform but because he or she is confident in his or her abilities to perform the job at hand. I'm not saying cops need to be perfect, but they must be there for their fellow Americans in times of crisis. In the end, that's why we all raised our hands and swore the oath.

The trait of love has to do with the love of one's fellow man. It is the fear of failing another human being. I remember responding to a "man down" call and when I got there it was a guy who had suffered a heart attack. I performed CPR, used an AED, the ambulance arrived, and I did not stop until the paramedics were ready to take over. Love turns into courage. Courage, to me, is when a person is scared but pushes on. When the Boston Marathon Bombings happened, what did we all witness on TV? We saw police officers, paramedics, and civilians getting the wounded out of harm's way. Fear was there but courage took over. That instinct to flee was pushed aside in order to help their fellow man. That is love.

Inevitably, at times, a police officer has to fight. A military member has to go to war. Fighting, to warriors, is the last resort and they must try everything in their power to avoid it. When someone with a warrior mindset is put in a spot where he has to act with violence, it will be done with effectiveness, ferociousness, and the fight will end quickly. 99% of cops out there do not want to fight or even pull their firearm out of their holsters. They would rather end things peacefully. In the end, everyone gets their day in court. It is unfortunately true that in some other countries citizens do not have the rights we have in the U.S.

To have a warrior mindset is to achieve a mental strength that allows someone to take on life's challenges through perseverance and sheer will. Is that so bad? Is that what the fear is? To have police officers with a warrior mindset? To be capable, confident, disciplined? The officer who adopts a warrior's mindset is not one to fear but one to be admired. That officer has compassion for his or her fellow man. The officer has traits like honor and love. The officer, even when afraid, pushes past that fear to help his or her fellow man.

The Thin Blue Line.
Image credit: Wikicommons

The word "warrior" should not be taboo in the law enforcement community. It should be adopted as a mindset, not as a ruthless fighter, but as a way of life.

THE ATTACK

I'm in my car
Traveling down the road
With the 1,000-yard stare.

My heart rate starts to rise,
Feelings of hyper-vigilance
Hit me like waves.

I grip the steering wheel tighter.
Faster and faster I go.
100 mph of speed
Equal to the beat of my heart.

I take deep breaths to slow it down,
So overwhelming as it hits its peak.
Where did this attack come from?
Could it be from my last operation?

Could it be from that IED strike decades ago?
Could it be from when I nearly pulled the trigger?

Haunted by the memories,
This attack won't be the only one.
It's the burden I bear.

21

COVID-19: A THIN BLUE LINE SEPARATES ORDER FROM CHAOS

"We suffer more often in imagination than in reality." —Seneca

COVID19 wreaked havoc everywhere. It shut the world down. It caused businesses to close. Lives were lost. But one thing didn't change and has increased: bad guys doing bad things. I'm not talking about speeders; I'm talking about hardened felons. In the law enforcement community, we had to stay out there, preventing crime and doing what we do. We are among those people who may have been infected with COVID-19 and may not have known. A majority of cops were not too concerned about the virus; they were more concerned about the rise of crime. They were concerned about unconstitutional rules set by politicians.

When COVID was first announced it was sometime at the end of February or the beginning of March 2020. Politicians allowed for only essential stores and personnel to be open. Are you ready for this?...to include liquor stores. During what was being called the deadliest virus in modern history, why were liquor stores allowed to stay open? Before I go on a rant about that, let's go over what has happened to law enforcement since the pandemic started.

Eventually, things started shutting down. Driving around, I felt like every day was a Sunday morning. As a plainclothes detective, it was very difficult for me to conduct any sort of operation against wanted felons because the only people that were out were cops, essential workers, and criminals. Now if you thought for a second that bad people with bad intentions cared anything about a pandemic, please go lock yourself in a closet and stay there. It was insane for me to see what was going on around me. Crime went up; bad guys were emboldened and then used the death of George Floyd to further their criminal enterprises. Again, I'm not talking about soccer mom speeders or very minor misdemeanors.

The Criminal Justice System

The next thing to close was our court system. So, if the court was closed, we couldn't make any arrests. Guess what happened after that? Crime went up, shootings, robberies, etc. I don't know what the politicians were thinking when all these rules were set in place. I got it, to limit the spread, but since when do bad guys truly care about not spreading a virus? It's like gun control, bad people with bad intentions will always get their hands on guns.

Once the courts closed, district attorneys across the country started releasing prisoners due to COVID-19. Defense attorneys called for their clients' release. Now, these felons were let out with conditions. Guess what started to happen-- the targeting of witnesses and old gang rivalries came back. There were all kinds of issues. We knew that would be a bad idea, but did anyone consult law enforcement? As far as I know, we were not consulted. Things were just done. Some district attorneys did a good job to prevent releasing certain felons. They let out only people with minor misdemeanors. Now it doesn't mean they were free, it just meant they had to show up to court for their trials.

Here's a quick story: My SWAT team was called to arrest a dangerous individual. This individual was an enforcer for a gang, and also connected to numerous shootings in the past. This individual was placed on a GPS bracelet. Now, it shouldn't come as too much of a surprise, this individual went right back to shooting, drug dealing, etc. Even with a GPS bracelet tied to him, he still went out and committed numerous felonies. The SWAT team was successful in taking this individual into custody.

After the death of George Floyd, one of the cops told the team to be careful because he had heard that a certain district attorney was looking to go after a cop. So, what does that mean, allow myself and my team to get shot by this suspect? Sorry, that's not the way I was brought up or trained. Here is the thing, after I made entry, I was number one through the door with my shield. The individual reached for his bed, where there was a Glock handgun. He surrendered as soon as he realized I had him already.

Now, let's think about this. Could I have discharged my firearm because of what this individual did? Absolutely. The individual was going for a handgun that would have placed me and the team in imminent danger. I did not need to though. By law, I would have been justified in the shoot, but to my morals, I was not justified. The individual knew I had the upper-hand and realized that giving up was the only option. Do you know how long it took to get to that decision not to shoot? Less than a second.

This felon we arrested was part of the COVID-19 release program, I'll just call it that. This individual and many others like them took full advantage of the shutdown and caused so much damage in the process.

Riots

The riots, or do I mean the peaceful protests? OK, there were peaceful protests, but what did the police deal with? The riots that are still going on. I believe that when you throw Molotov cocktails and IEDs at cops, you have now become an insurgency. You are no longer labeled a protestor or rioter; no, you've crossed the line. So even with all this lockdown talk by our fearless political officials, they stated that they couldn't infringe on individuals' rights to free speech. Now, people weren't allowed to go to church (or church had to be held outside with everyone socially distant.)

But let's have a riot. It's all good.

Here is another story: One of our officers died a year or so ago. A motorcycle rally and a fundraiser were to be held for the officer's family. The group was denied a permit. So, they changed the name of the fundraiser and called it a protest to "back the blue." The permits were approved. It was both humorous and sad at the same time.

COVID-19 rules got so out of hand that people were calling 911 if they saw someone outside not wearing a mask. A majority of police departments across the country would not enforce those rules because of a document called The U.S. Constitution.

My job is to uphold and defend the constitution, not use my power to infringe on an individual's rights to privacy.

COVID-19 brought out people's stupidity as well as their resilience to adapt and overcome this situation. Some people did not allow a virus to stop them from living, while others were so scared, they refused to leave their houses.

For us, in the military and first responder community, we did not have a choice. I have gone into homes where disease was everywhere. I have dealt with people who had the flu, MRSA, the alphabet of hepatitis, and numerous other diseases. I probably wouldn't have been infected, but anything is possible. Yet the point is, we still go. To us, it doesn't matter with, but the point is, we still go.

To us, the line between order and chaos is thin and blue.

22

FERGUSON TO MINNEAPOLIS: WHAT'S GOING ON WITH LAW ENFORCEMENT?

"To use physical force only when the exercise of persuasion, advice and warning is found to be insufficient to obtain public cooperation to an extent necessary to secure observance of law or to restore order, and to use only the minimum degree of physical force which is necessary on any particular occasion for achieving a police objective."—Sir Robert Peel

As I stood in formation on day one of the police academy, I thought to myself: "Here we go again..." I was reminded of Army boot camp. The Drill instructors, on day one, were all over us. Yelling in our faces, inducing stress, watching how we reacted. It was the same on day one of the academy.

"Here we go again..."

Fast forward 6 months later, I graduated from the police academy. I looked at my brand-new badge on the upper left side of my chest.

There was a sense of honor, accomplishment, a similar feeling I had when graduating boot camp. I have always been the type that when the national anthem is played, a tingle runs down my spine. I feel a sudden burst of love for the country and the people I fought for. To some, this might sound cliché. To those like me, it is a calling for a higher purpose.

Throughout the years I've been a police officer, I have dealt with all sorts of people. Some of them are the worst in society while others are victims of circumstance. There is one thing I'd like to touch on though…What is going on with law enforcement? It is a loaded question. Not that I have the solution, but there is a point that needs discussing.

In the year 2020, George Floyd died due to the actions of police officers there. Is it an issue of race? Training? Leadership? I can't know what was going on in the officer's head. What I, and the law enforcement community can do, is speak up when one of our own has done something wrong. Police chiefs and officers around the country have already spoken out against the officer and his conduct.

The media makes it seem that police officers around the country are running wild, shooting up unarmed black men. This couldn't be further from the truth. 99% of police officers around the country do the right thing. They enforce the law. They protect the public. They are everyday heroes in a very thankless job.

People want to place blame on the law enforcement community. Again, the media makes it seem like most police officers are rabid dogs out there hurting the public. What do statistics from the Department of Justice show?

"An estimated 62.9 million U.S. residents age 16 or older, or about 26 percent of the population, had one or more contacts with police in 2011, the Justice Department's Bureau of Justice Statistics (BJS) announced today.

Contact between police and the public was equally likely to be initiated by residents as by police. About half (51 percent) of police contacts occurred when persons requested police assistance, while the other half (49 percent) were police initiated, such as when police pulled over drivers during traffic stops or stopped persons in public places but not a moving vehicle (i.e., street stops).

The majority of persons with police contact believed the police behaved properly. In 2011, 93 percent of those who requested police assistance, 88 percent of drivers pulled over in traffic stops, and 71 percent of persons involved in street stops thought the police behaved properly during the contact. Regardless of the reason for the contact, less than 5 percent of persons who did not believe the police had behaved properly filed a complaint.

Black drivers (13 percent) were more likely than Whites (10 percent) and Hispanics (10 percent) to be pulled over by police in a traffic stop; however, Blacks, Whites, and Hispanics were equally likely to be stopped in a street stop (less than one percent each). Among those involved in street or traffic stops, Blacks were less likely than Whites and Hispanics to believe the police behaved properly during the encounter."

Another area people tend to blame is police training. I have seen police department budgets get slashed; the result is training falls back and other programs that help police officers perform their jobs better and safer are cut. Some police departments allow officers to go to the range only once or twice a year. Police departments conduct other training such as CPR/AED, Legal Updates, and other types of training once a year. It all depends on what they are allowed to spend the money on.

Is it really about race? Or lack of training? My family once pointed out to me that when I describe a situation that occurred at work. I never say, "This Black guy I dealt with, this Mexican guy I dealt with, this White guy I dealt with." My description is always, "This asshole I dealt with..." That gave me a moment of pause. I had to really think about it. They were right. To me, a bad guy is a bad guy. I don't see race. I just see the crime that was committed.

One area of concern I don't hear too much about is the applicants that show up to take the test, pass and then apply to become a police officer. I have seen a steady decline in qualified candidates over the years. I blame society. When politicians stand up and blame an entire profession, when the media portrays law enforcement as reckless, when certain incentives such as education bonuses are cut, it really has an impact on those who show interest in becoming police officers. The police departments are forced to hire less qualified individuals.

How about good cops going after a bad cop? I hear this a lot, "Well, why don't you turn these bad ones in." Most of the time, the bad ones do get dealt with. They either get fired, indicted for various crimes, or both. I've seen officers get written up for various issues, get suspended, and eventually lose their jobs. A cop that other cops can't trust does not last long. The few that slip through the cracks, unfortunately, eventually get caught and it's usually for something big.

Early in my career, I was working in the booking room at my police department. A good friend and fellow academy graduate brought in an arrest from the stadium. It was a police officer. The officer was belligerent to borderline combative. The officer was arrested because he was caught urinating in public. These are things we deal with all the time, with drunks at a concert or sporting event. If we arrested every single person that urinated on a wall, the jail cells would be completely full. They usually get a summons to court, get kicked out of the game and a lifetime ban from the stadium. This individual decided to identify themselves as a cop and then call my friend, "Oh, OK Obama, OK

Obama." The off-duty officer continued to berate the officer, and that behavior led to his arrest.

The next day, the officer's chief of police came to my department and personally apologized for his officer's conduct. The chief was embarrassed, his shoulders were slouched, I could tell he was disgusted by the behavior of one of his own officers. A few days later, we learned the officer was terminated. I don't know what happened to his court case, but that particular ex-cop will never be allowed to wear a badge again. So, bad cops do get dealt with. They do end up in serious trouble and are often fired or arrested.

One thing that a lot of cops, when dealing with a situation, always ask: Does the punishment fit the crime? As in, depending on the crime or situation, does it warrant a certain response? For example, I was sent to a fight in progress, my level of adrenaline was high, and I was prepared to arrest someone or be forced to use some type of force if my commands weren't obeyed. There are several things that need to happen if I was to use any force. Sometimes they go in order, other times it goes right to the extreme. Volatile situations are extremely unpredictable, so these decisions happen in seconds. The steps I am talking about are called The Use of Force Continuum. Officers must follow their department policies and procedures. There isn't any discretion allowed; they must be followed. The process goes something like this:

- Officer Presence — No force is used. Considered the best way to resolve a situation.
- The mere presence of a law enforcement officer works to deter crime or diffuse a situation.
- Officers' attitudes are professional and nonthreatening.
- Verbalization — Force is not physical.
- Officers issue calm, nonthreatening commands, such as "Let me see your identification and registration."
- Officers may increase their volume and shorten commands in an attempt to gain compliance. Short commands might include "Stop," or "Don't move."

- Empty-Hand Control — Officers use bodily force to gain control of a situation.
- Soft technique. Officers use grabs, holds, and joint locks to restrain an individual.
- Hard technique. Officers use punches and kicks to restrain an individual.
- Less-Lethal Methods — Officers use less-lethal technologies to gain control of a situation.
- Blunt impact. Officers may use a baton or projectile to immobilize a combative person.
- Chemical. Officers may use chemical sprays or projectiles embedded with chemicals to restrain an individual (e.g., pepper spray).
- Conducted Energy Devices (CEDs). Officers may use CEDs to immobilize an individual. CEDs discharge a high-voltage, low-amperage jolt of electricity at a distance.
- Lethal Force — Officers use lethal weapons to gain control of a situation. Should only be used if a suspect poses a serious threat to the officer or another individual.
- Officers use deadly weapons such as firearms to stop an individual's actions.
  (*Source:* National Institute of Justice, "The Use-of-Force Continuum," August 3, 2009)

So did the punishment fit the crime in 2020 in Minneapolis? Most reports state that Mr. Floyd did not resist the officers. Media reports also state that the witness video was eight minutes long and shows an officer using a technique that is not supposed to be used. On top of that, the crime was passing forged currency. The rule of thumb is, once the handcuffs are on the fight is done. If the suspect is still fighting, then there are other restraints that can be applied, or a different transport vehicle could arrive to take the combative suspect.

This profession is hard enough as it is. Add the above statements to the mix and you get some overworked, stressed good cops. I've heard it all, "You signed up for this…" Exactly, I did. I went into this profession fully acknowledging the dangers it poses, the mental and emotional heartache it creates. I accept that one day I may die; war taught me that. I will do my job and continue to do my job with honor, integrity, courage, and all the virtues that come with it. I will fight if I'm forced to. I will protect lives. I will treat others with respect. I will honor the sacrifices of those before me. This is just not me saying it. It is the 99% who put on that shield every day and face the unknown.

REALITY OF THE JOB

Every door I knock on is mostly bad news.
Most cars I stop, I don't plan on giving a ticket.
It's either to tell them to slow down.
or tell them their taillight is out.
When I go order a meal
I try to go to places where
I see my food being made.
When I eat, my back is to the wall.
Head on a swivel,
Is my food poisoned?
Spit on?
Was this the restaurant
where that pedophile worked I arrested?
I constantly scan for threats,
whether going to a call
Driving on the road,
or even stopped taking a quick lunch
break in my car,
Constant 911 calls,
Domestic Violence,
The wife who called 911 is now fighting
My partner and me because
She doesn't want her abusive spouse to go to jail.
Murders,
The smell hits you,
You try to keep your composure.
Child Abuse,

God, I want to punch this
fuck in the face.
Fatal accidents,
Notify parents
their child is no longer here.
Heart Attacks,
CPR, C'mon man breathe!
Elder Abuse,
Rape in progress,
I hope to God
I get there to get this sick fuck.
Shooting in progress,
Lock and load, put on my SWAT kit, armed barricade.
Active break ins,
Random scream in the night,
Adrenaline is pumping.
Tones going off in your car,
Dispatch frantic "clear the air."
Officer in trouble,
Shit I just spoke to him a minute ago,
I go home at the end of the night,
Take a deep breath,
My family has its needs,
Bills to pay,
Mouths to feed,
My son/daughter wants to play,
I feel distant, I need a minute,
Head to bed, can't sleep.
Do it all over again tomorrow.

23

PROPER LAW ENFORCEMENT TRAINING REQUIRES "REFUNDING THE POLICE"

The hardship of the exercises is intended less to strengthen the back than to toughen the mind. The Spartans say that any army may win while it still has its legs under it; the real test comes when all strength is fled and the men must produce victory on will alone." — Steven Pressfield

Police Officers are shuffled through their respective police training academies. Academy training can last anywhere from 6 weeks to 6 months depending on where you are in the United States. In previous articles, I have argued that police officers do not train enough in academies or throughout their careers. Most proactive police officers end up seeking out other training to improve their skillsets. Most of this training is costly and, depending on the agency, they may have to use personal time to attend.

Over the years, I've discovered high-level training courses and research papers dealing with human performance as well as neurological, physiological, psychological, and biomechanical effects. Several companies dive into the biggest questions of all: the "why" behind a Use of Force incident, the "why" behind cognitive interviewing, tunnel vision, and many other "whys" that we are continuing to be researched to this day.

The psychological aspect of policing is one of the most important parts of the job. Confidence is a large part of the psychological process. This doesn't include being conceited or arrogant, but rather being confident in yourself, in your abilities, and your knowledge. I see time and time again that cops cannot decide whether to arrest or to summons in the case of simple crimes. I've repeatedly seen situations in which an officer clams up in front of an unruly person. They suffer from stimulus overload. Is it a training issue? I believe it is.

The quote by LTC Grossman that "*The sense of personal effectiveness and self-confidence created by realistic training is as much a stress reducer as when the muscles go on autopilot*" is 100% accurate. The best training for any police officer is realistic Force on Force training. Force on Force means shoot or don't shoot. An officer is inserted into a scenario with full duty gear, as well as SIMS equipment (retrofitting the officer's duty weapon with a different bolt that shoots out "paintball" bullets.) During the training scenario the officer must "respond" to a domestic disturbance, fight, suspicious person, and all kinds of other situations. The officer must make decisions, sometimes under crisis. The officer's heart rate is raised, a lot of stimuli are thrown at him or her, and through that fog of chaos the officer is tasked with re-shaping the situation to observe, orient, decide and act. Yes, the good old OODA Loop.

Officers must have the confidence to do the job. Confidence is developed through reality-based training. It's not just about stress inoculation. A police trainer can put officers through stress inoculation scenarios, but the most important part of this type of training is teaching officers how THEY react when exposed to stress. Officers must recognize how they are affected by stress psychologically and physiologically.

The next part of police training is neurological and deals with the mind, eyes, ears and other senses and the ability to read threats and make sound judgments. Sure, this can be lumped in with the psychological but I'm talking about the brain--the complex human brain and all the receptors involved. Research conducted by Force Science Institute shows that a suspect can draw a pistol from their waistband, point, and shoot in an average of .25 seconds. The research also shows that after the initial shot, each subsequent shot will average another .25 seconds.

Force Science Institute also tested the reaction time of officers. They started with a simple experiment. The officer sees a light blink on, then the officer shoots. This was a simple no stress-induced test. They discovered it took an officer .31 seconds to shoot. The more complex the experiment the more time it took for the officer to shoot. The average time was .83 seconds to fire. In literally a split second, an officer must process a suspect's actions by reading body language, observing hands, recognizing a gun or knife, and address the threat. This all must be executed in under a second.

The calls by certain politicians, groups, and others for an officer to "shoot the legs" is nearly impossible and defies all logic considering the neurological load and stimuli officers are subject to. Officers must assess, decide and act on the information in front of them. The following simple task illustrates this point.

A driver pulls up to a traffic light. The light turns yellow, and that observation causes one of two things. The driver slows down and prepares to stop or speeds up to beat the red light. How long did all that take? That entire scenario was less than a second: Observe, orient, decide, and act. Studying the human brain and all its complexities is vital to police officers and should be included in training. Officers need to know how their brains function under stress and must experience their reactions to learn this. Such training is extremely rare and typically does not occur in most police departments.

"Regular aerobic exercise, reduction of time spent each day in sedentary activities, dietary habits that promote heart health, and exercise that helps strengthen muscles around joints may help overcome these disparities, these recommendations can be challenging to consistently implement on a daily basis. Challenging, but worth the effort!" -Dr. Rod Pope

Human Performance and physical fitness are critical to this job. There is a great deal of research out there for athletes about human performance, including VO2 max readings, heart rate, blood pressure, etc. and it's incumbent on each officer to seek out this research. I've seen too many cops, after the police academy, just let themselves go due to the demands of the job. Some police departments are better than others at addressing officers' physical fitness. At the end of the day, it is up to the officer to engage in these programs.

Lack of sleep affects human performance. Police officers are in a profession that does not allow for a lot of sleep, especially for the rookies. They can kiss sleep goodbye. Is it because the agency is that busy? Yes, but it's also about manpower. There are never enough cops working the streets to address the needs of the citizens. But how does lack of sleep hurt the officer?

A study conducted by the University of Chicago revealed that sleeping only four hours a night can impact young adults to the point that some develop glucose and insulin characteristics of diabetics. According to the National Sleep Foundation, inadequate sleep causes lower levels of appetite along with depressing the amounts of regulating hormones in the body, resulting in more eating and weight gain.

"Fatigue from sleep deprivation robs officers not only of a sense of personal wellbeing but also profoundly affects the cognitive abilities vital to their survival—alertness, decision-making, resilience from stress. So when we talk about counter-fatigue measures, we're talking potentially about life-or-death implications."-Dr. Bill Lewenski

A research project involving the Royal Canadian Mounted Police in which over 40 volunteers took part in an anti-fatigue study found that, after several weeks, fatigue management training improved police sleep, health, and overall wellness.

Specialized training for law enforcement officers is needed. It's more than a want: It is a need. Proper training must be implemented from the moment an officer goes to the academy to the moment he or she retires. Officers must learn more about themselves and how they react to crises. Only then can they respond accordingly. Police training budgets must be increased. States, cities, and towns must invest in their officers.

After all, at times, it is a life-and-death situation.

24

WILL RACISM EVER DIE?

I was born in Monrovia, Liberia, in the western part of Africa. I lived there until I was about 7 years old. A civil war broke out there around 1988. My family had to leave. My last memory of Liberia was a soldier jumping out of the back of a truck and then getting blown up by a grenade.

In Lebanon, it wasn't any better. Civil war still ravaged the land. I remember artillery rounds hitting the side of a small mountain near the village my family is from. If memory serves, we made our way to the U.S. in the winter of 1989.

Since I was not a born citizen of the U.S., I became a naturalized citizen in 2006 after coming home from the Iraq war. My great-grandparents were African. I have family that are African, Lebanese and American. My experiences in my early years in other parts of the world and in the U.S. shaped me. It made me resilient. Why share a little history of my family? To set the stage for what I'm going to discuss.

Will racism ever die?

I've been spat at, ridiculed, threatened, even gotten into fights over my race. I've been called names regarding my skin color, been called names because people thought I was Mexican or Puerto Rican. I was called names because of my African and Middle Eastern heritage. Did I ever let it get to me? Did I ever allow myself to be soured by it? Did I cast blame on an entire race of people? No. I have seen what it's like to hate. I have seen what it's like to be so full of hate, that you are willing to kill for it. I used those experiences as fuel for the fire that burned in me. Not once though did I blame a race. There are, in my own family, some racist individuals. That never did pass onto me. I was always the type that if I was treated with respect, I would give it back.

Lately, for the past decade I'd say, talk of racism has been on an uptick. Whether it's police brutality, white on black crimes, white on Arab crimes, and the list goes on.

Humans historically have been tribal. Take a look around, right here in the U.S. There are entire communities of the same races. Asian, Middle Eastern, Italian, and so much more.

Author Sebastian Junger said it best, "If you want to make a society work, then you don't keep underscoring the places where you're different—you underscore your shared humanity." Before my unit mobilized to Iraq in 2005, we had to go through some cultural training. I recall one soldier having a problem with not being allowed to speak to a woman in Iraq. That was the culture. He still could not fathom that thought. I had to explain to him that it's just the way it is. They aren't American and they are a totally different culture. Was that racism? No, that was just not understanding the culture. Most of our racism, I believe, is because we don't understand certain types of people.

In the military, when I was at boot camp, I was surrounded by every religion, race, and creed that America had to offer. I remember one day, before we loaded the cattle cars (cattle cars are literally as they sound, except recruits were put in them) in Fort Sill, Oklahoma. All of us agreed to say a prayer. A Christian, a Jew and a Muslim all said a prayer. I was the Muslim. It was surreal to me and went against what my family and culture taught me. Americans hate everyone. They are divided. They do not accept anyone. That couldn't have been further from the truth. Deep inside I knew it. It gave me more motivation to fight for us. To fight for the idea of a free America.

As I stated before though, we are human, we are shaped by our experiences. Some are not easily swayed while others are. In the end, because we are human, we are prone to biases, stereotypes and straight out racist thoughts. For example, even though I have great-grandparents who are African, I have family members who hate Africans. It is mind-boggling to me.

I see politicians and community leaders who promise to get rid of racism. That is a fallacy. I have seen Africans hate each other because of being from different tribes; in Lebanon, Iraq and various other parts of the Middle East, Shiites hate Sunni Muslims and vice versa. Now comes the question, "Well, what does this have to do with the U.S.?" In the U.S., we have a mix of every culture, religion, color, etc. Those biases, racism and stereotypes come with that mix.

While I was in the military, I learned that it wasn't about race. It was about the person to the left and right of you. That made a difference between living or dying on the battlefield. Soldiers fought for each other, cried to together, laughed together. It did not matter. Soldiers bled one color. Green. Why can't civilians learn that? Why can't the rest of America take a page out of the U.S. military and work together? It is a difficult question. Only when we as Americans are tested do we show our true colors. I remember, after 9/11, we were all waving the flag of the U.S. We joined the military, we fought for America. We fought for our freedoms. That was our generation's moment.

In the end, even though I had to deal with racism on a personal level, it never shaped me. It never made me hate another race. I will not blame the majority because of a minority. That minority is the one I'd rather deal with. That minority, who are cowards, who try to run people like my mother off the road because she dresses a certain way. We are all Americans. United we stand. Divided we fall.

25

SIFTING THROUGH THE MEDIA BIAS: A COP'S PERSPECTIVE ON USING SOCIAL WORKERS

In one form or another, police reform has been occurring all across the country. Some states have instituted drastic changes that emboldened the criminal element of their major cities such as Chicago, Portland, Seattle, and others. One of the recommended reforms was having social workers accompany police officers or assigning social workers to police departments. The NYPD is one of the police departments that has implemented a city-wide pilot program that prohibits police officers from responding to mental health calls in parts of Manhattan. This all sounds great on paper. Here are the facts:

I read an article by Nicole Johnson and Lauren Cook of ABC local news 10 in New York. The following is an excerpt:

"Police responses to some calls in the city have escalated to violence or even death, including the shooting deaths of Miguel Richards, Susan

Muller, and Deborah Danner. All of them suffered from mental illness and were shot by NYPD officers during encounters inside their homes.

Mayor Bill De Blasio said the COVID pandemic has made the importance of mental health—and how emergency calls are addressed—clearer than ever. "If a family is in crisis, and it's not a situation involving violence, we are going to send civilians to address those calls."

Let's look at each of those names and get the facts. Let's start with Miguel Richards. Police were called and were allowed inside the Richards' apartment. Police reported that he had a knife in his left hand and his right hand was behind him. They repeatedly told him to drop the knife. A team of backup officers arrived with a stun gun. An officer noticed a gun that Miguel was trying to conceal behind his back. Miguel then raised the gun and pointed it at the officers. Officers opened fire. To me, this looks like a classic suicide by cop, an extremely dangerous situation. This was all caught on bodycam.

Police fatally shot Susan Muller after she called 911 and then lunged at responding officers with a 10-inch knife. The NYPD reported they did not know why she lunged at the officers with a knife but there had been repeated 911 calls in the past to her residence.

Concerning Deborah Danner, NYPD responded for an emotionally disturbed person (EDP) in a 7th-floor apartment. Sgt Hugh Barry testified that when he arrived at the apartment, Danner was on her bed angrily cutting up the paper with scissors. He said he tried to persuade her to come out to see a medic, but she refused, slamming the scissors down on a nightstand and standing just outside the door.

That's when Barry said she ran back into her room and grabbed a baseball bat. "She was too fast for me," Barry said. "The last thing I wanted was for her to go into the room and get the scissors." Barry said he drew his gun and pleaded with her to drop the bat, but she stepped toward him. "I just see the bat swinging and that's when I fired," he said. "I'm looking at this bat that can crack me in the head and kill me." That's when he opened fire, killing Danner.

Before I get messages about how it was "just a bat," consider the case of Sgt Michael Chesna who was killed in Weymouth, Massachusetts by an EDP who had committed various crimes. The EDP threw a rock at Sgt Chesna's head, knocking him out. The EDP then went up to Sgt Chesna, grabbed his service weapon, and shot him repeatedly at point-blank range. The EDP then killed an elderly lady standing outside of her home who just happened to witness the carnage.

In the quote above, the reporter used those three names as examples. I feel those are poor examples. Not only did the reporter not give all the facts, but she made it seem that they were all non-violent encounters. Would the presence of a social worker change the circumstances? Or would sending unarmed social workers only and not police to each of those situations result in a different outcome?

I began a program at my police department in which a social worker is assigned to our unit once a week. They are a great resource to have. I go around my city addressing the mental health needs of individuals and families who do not know what is available for them. It has been successful so far to help bridge that gap between law enforcement and mental health. It makes it much easier to navigate the mental health world. I've been able to direct families through the mental health system. These experiences have made me realize how broken that system is.

Here is a misconception that most people believe: the social worker will de-escalate an already volatile situation. This is an extremely difficult task. At times, an EDP is so far gone, that some sort of Use of Force, will occur. In the end, it is also about the preservation of life. When an EDP is suicidal, they are also potentially homicidal in order to get the police to shoot them. But again, these are extreme cases, and most times, these incidents are resolved peacefully by the police officer.

In the world where 80% of cops are just there to collect a paycheck and 20% are actually doing the job, it's that 20% that have the gift of gab that can get the most hardened criminal or EDP to comply easily. The 20% are reasonable, they care, they apply the skillset to their everyday life. The 20% can diffuse a situation by merely showing up, taking charge, and talking it out with the individual. Some of the best cops I know are ones that are able to resolve 99% of situations peacefully.

A social worker was not there to "de-escalate." It was done by officers who understand human nature and apply it to their daily patrols.

Having social workers attached to police departments is a positive change. It is another tool to address society's issues. It shouldn't be left to police officers to wear multiple hats throughout the course of their duties. It's hard enough as it is. Adding the mental health issues around the country has been extremely taxing on police departments in terms of man-hours.

KEEP GOING

My head hangs low
Breathing heavy
Heart rate high
Memories flowing,
I close my eyes
As the sweat drips down my face.
Keep going
I say to myself.

I rub some chalk on my hands.
I grip the bar and feel the texture.
My mind connected to my body.

My feet are rooted to the ground beneath.
I solidify my body,
my will,
my resolve,
I squeeze the bar,
brace and lift.
Every inch I lift the bar
I feel my muscles tighten
Until I hit the top of the lift.
I then lower the bar.
I sit down,
My head hangs low.
Breathing heavy

Heart rate high
Memories flowing
Beads of sweat drip down my face.
Each bead of sweat is my pain
Each bead of sweat is my rage
Each bead of sweat is for me
To fight another day.
Workout done,
Demons tired.
I push forward
For those we lost.
I push forward
For my brothers in arms.

26

COPS HAVE BEEN SCREAMING FOR CRIMINAL JUSTICE REFORM

Criminal Justice Reform has been a topic of discussion and outright anger by many law enforcement agencies. Officers have been killed by individuals who should not be out of jail. Victims of domestic violence get hurt again and again by their abusers because they were let out early. More recently, due to COVID-19, judges were releasing some violent individuals back to society, and surprise, surprise, they were reoffending. In addition to the issue of early release, we have been fighting for more mental health care. Our officers are inundated with mental health calls. These two subjects, early release and mental health, must be addressed.

Let's start with the revolving door of justice. I have personally arrested some violent offenders only to have them come right back out on the streets to re-offend. This became even more prevalent with the onset of COVID. Judges have allowed the release of violent offenders in my neck of the woods, and there has been an uptick in shootings, gang violence, homicides, witness intimidation, and a whole host of other problems.

How are we going to fix this? As law enforcement, we enforce laws that are passed by legislatures that represent the people. The people who want these laws expect the police to enforce them. Now, this would be true in a perfect world. The reality is that some laws are passed because politicians are trying to be re-elected, or because they have personal agendas, etc. If the legislatures truly worked for the people, then certain laws would not have passed, and violent offenders would not be released so quickly.

I'm going to discuss a case I worked involving a sexual predator. (I am going to keep it vague to protect the victim.) This guy was a bad guy. His modus operandi (MO) was to gain the trust of a family, which included mentally disabled individuals, and target the kids. He preyed upon them. He was patient and he waited, like the predator that he was. The mother of the child walked in on him after he abused her child. I am not going to describe what he did to the victim.

Let's fast forward a little. This predator kept harassing the family after he found out they filed a police report. He followed them around all over the city. We were able to arrest him and charge him accordingly. I then learned he was released and did not understand why. I was angry about it because the very system that is supposed to protect the victims has failed miserably. The predator then took off somewhere down south because the court allowed him to do so. I did not know this, they failed to notify me. A case that should have taken about a year or so took three years to clear. I finally tracked him down, requested a warrant, and arrested him. He was later convicted and sent to jail for a long time.

There are so many cases like the one I described above.

Let's move on to mental health. There is a real crisis with mental health exacerbated by the shutdown of state hospitals due to budget cuts and a whole host of other reasons. This caused a lot of issues. So many people who suffer from mental illness are now not getting the help they need. Many of them are prone to violence and they self-medicate with illegal drugs. Too often families of those with mental illnesses are unable to find help for their loved ones.

I once had to investigate a report of several cars that had been damaged by a person, we will call "X", who was suffering from mental health issues. X took a large rock and started bashing car windows, hoods, sunroofs, etc. A woman was sitting in her car when this was happening, and she stated that he was laughing like a maniac. I eventually arrested him and charged him with a series of crimes. X's parents were at their wit's end with him. They told me they tried everything to get X admitted somewhere. They knew he was a danger to the public. Unfortunately, there wasn't room in any facilities for him. As a result, X kept being released. This person would be declared competent to stand trial, but jail is not the right environment for him.

Criminal Justice reform is just one part of the equation. There are so many other factors. Police officers today wear many hats. What the public that we serve must determine is what they want from their police departments and present that to their elected officials. In the end, the police represent the people of their respective communities.

And always remember this: police officers are a reflection of the society they serve.

27

THE HALF MEASURE MINDSET HAS NO PLACE IN POLICE WORK

It seems that these days, police officers everywhere are rated by statistics. How many cars have they pulled over? How many citations? How many arrests? The list goes on and on. Police departments start looking more and more like a business rather than a public service, generating revenue for states, cities, and towns rather than policing the community.

This situation causes officers to have a half-measure mindset, which to me is doing just enough to get by. Writing enough citations so the officer doesn't get called on the carpet. Getting enough arrests so the officer is not on the command staff's radar. OK, so this is going to be another frank discussion that may hurt some feelings, but hey, it needs to be said.

Over 10 years ago, I worked for a PD that monitored the state's transit system. I was assigned to the plainclothes anti-crime unit. Now, being in plain clothes allowed me to do some quite amusing people watching. My lord, the things I've seen people do in the transit system. Let's put it this way, I wouldn't sit on any seats, I wouldn't hold on to any poles or railings unless I was in MOPP level 4. (For the non-military reader, Mission Oriented Protective Posture (MOPP) level 4 is protective gear for a toxic environments like radioactive, chemical, biological, and even nuclear. MOPP level 4 has you covered.) So, you can imagine how I feel about the transit system in this country and the world.

Back to my story. I was sitting on a bench, kind of resting my head back against the billboard, pretending to be "out of it." I noticed three individuals walking down to the platform and they were openly talking about making a drug deal. I discreetly signaled to my fellow plainclothes officers to move closer. We all got on the train. I told one of them what I had observed and came up with a game plan.

So long story short, we observed the drug exchange, arrested all parties involved, job well done by all. A few days later, I was questioned by my supervisor as to why my smoking citation numbers were down.

I looked at him and asked, "Are you serious?" In my mind, I knew it wasn't coming from him but the command staff on the second floor. Instead of doing what I was supposed to as an undercover officer in the transit system, I was told to write more citations. In the end, I was expected to be a revenue generator for the transit system.

I hated it and decided to go back to uniform patrol. Don't get me wrong, looking at officer productivity is important. A chief or commander can tell who their workers are and who their slackers are. Tell me what's better: an officer who arrests bad guys, protects and serves, and issues citations when necessary versus an officer whose sole concern is the number of tickets issued.

I'm not saying police departments are forcing quotas because that is illegal, and I hope in this day and age no department is doing quotas. But some, or perhaps most, departments are rating their officers based on numbers--not on quality policing but quantity. Believe me, I could pull over three cars and one of them would have a driver who is a complete asshole and deserves a ticket.

Now you have some officers running around just trying to keep their "numbers" up and not looking at the big picture. For example, a person gets pulled over for a red-light violation. The officer issues the citation and lets the driver go. However, the officer misses several important details: 1) the person is sweating when it is winter, 2) the person never looks at the officer, or 3) the person keeps looking at their center console as if they are hiding something in there. All the behavioral cues were missed because the officer was only thinking about the next ticket, to stay "off the boss's radar." This is a half-measure mindset and is creating officers who concern themselves with "numbers" rather than quality policing.

Now, the officers who come with the full measure warrior mind-set do not thrive well in those environments. These officers are your true workers in those departments. They are outside-the-box thinkers. They solve crimes, they engage with the community, they do far more for the department than the command staff truly knows. They don't ask for recognition, just the ability to do police work without the cloud of "numbers" hanging over their heads. These cops are a full measure, they come with first, second, and third-order effects in a community. The half-measure officers do not mesh well with these officers. While the half-measure officers worry about their numbers, the full measure cops are working on preventing crime.

Full measure officers always joke and poke fun at the half- measure officers. "Yeah, you write a ticket for an expired sticker but never mind the dead person in the backseat of the car." If you are reading this, and you are a cop, you've probably already thought of several fellow officers who fit this description.

Half-measure policing is not good for the community. It causes hard-working officers to concern themselves with numbers rather than the quality-of-life issues in their city or town. The community doesn't need a half- measure cop. The community needs the officer who is the full measure, the one who has a warrior mindset, the one who cares.

28

EGO IS THE #1 COP-KILLER

"You have power over your mind - not outside events. Realize this, and you will find strength."— *Marcus Aurelius*

We always hear about what kills a police officer. Gunfire, suicide, fatal accidents, heart attacks, and on and on. Each death is painful, each death is a lost brother or sister in blue. Police departments across the nation grieve and they hold massive wakes and funerals to honor their respective police officers.

We wear black mourning bands around our badges to signify what we lost. Do you know what factor goes into some of these painful scenarios? Ego. Ego is a huge issue in the police profession and truly stands out in policing. It will come back on an egotistical officer through civilian complaints, arrests when it wasn't warranted, quick tempers, grievances, etc.

When young cops are molded by egotistical veteran field training officers (FTOs), they are in for a rough career if they choose to emulate their training officer. I was fortunate enough that all my FTOs were good cops and checked their egos at the door when they entered their respective cruisers. I could tell immediately that they had a warrior mindset. They had the mindset to perform the job and perform it well.

As a young cop, I found it refreshing that there were cops like that. I grew up dealing with some of the most egotistical assholes that had the power to arrest. I remember being yelled at by officers several times as a kid. I have seen egotistical officers lose their minds at the simplest of insults.

When I was in high school, around 16 years old, I remember that an officer approached one of my friends who was smoking a cigarette in the school parking lot. The officer told him to put it out. In the town where I lived it was illegal to smoke outdoors, which was ridiculous to me. I got that he was underage, but it was the officer's approach to my friend that upset him. He called the officer an asshole as he was driving away.

The officer then slammed on his brakes, whipped his cruiser around, got out, and began to scream at my friend. I can't repeat what he said but I remember there were plenty of F-bombs. We were subjected to quite the treatment.

When you work in the profession, you realize that some officers never left that high school football team mentality. You know that prepubescent egotistical jock mentality. Walking into a football locker room is like walking into the lion's den. If you don't belong there, you will know it. If you insult them, you will either get beaten up or picked on.

One of the most dangerous situations I have ever seen involved police supervisors. Some of them are extremely egotistical. Some of them subscribe to an authoritarian style of leadership in which an individual has complete control over all decisions and little to no input from subordinates. An example of this leadership style is something I'll never forget. I have to be extremely vague due to operational security but you will get the gist.

A massive operation was being formulated to take down some heavy hitters. Heavy hitters are extremely violent, dangerous felons, and the probability of a shootout is extremely high. There were multiple search warrants and arrest warrants for various members of a criminal organization. My SWAT team was tasked with going after the leader of this group who was the most violent of all of them. As this plan was being formulated, I was asked, as a SWAT assistant team leader, for suggestions.

I advised the detective on how SWAT could handle the situation and what resources would be needed to pull off an arrest without incident. The biggest part of the operation was that we couldn't risk doing a middle of the night hit due to the arsenal the leader had in the residence. So, I decided to take down the leader while in his vehicle. The street was perfect due to how narrow it was, which would decrease the likelihood of the leader attempting to flee. With the plans in place, I left for the day.

Later that week I found out that the supervisor of the operation did not want to do my plan and wanted to handle the leader. He ended up planning the takedown of the leader himself with a couple of his minions. It was an awful plan that involved taking this leader in a parking lot. I could already foresee civilians getting caught in the crossfire, and I could already see that the leader would escape. I could see a multitude of issues.

To me, and most other officers, a vehicle takedown is extremely dangerous. A car is a 2,000 pound weapon. It is like a missile coming at you. I've had friends get seriously hurt by bad guys hitting them while trying to escape.

On the day of the takedown, I voiced my concerns. I did not like their plan nor did the team leader. The rule of thumb is, when you call SWAT, you let SWAT plan the operation, and a supervisor can sit back and watch them work from the command center. This supervisor's ego was so big that it did not matter. The supervisor wanted to plan it, without consulting with any of the SWAT leadership.

The criminal mastermind left the residence, and SWAT made its way to his house. They gained entry and secured it for the investigating detectives so they could come in and process all the evidence. We found a short barrel AK-47 with a magazine in the weapon. It was locked and loaded, ready to go, as it was with most of the other guns we found. As SWAT was clearing the scene, I heard on the radio, "BROKE CONTAINMENT, BROKE CONTAINMENT."

I said it out loud. "I KNEW IT." It turned into a 20-minute pursuit. The leader was being tracked by an air unit. The officers kept their distance as a result. The leader got out of the vehicle and ran into the woods. Now, this turned into a search in the woods. Eventually, the leader was caught. The supervisor and his team were high fiving each other, pleased at their work. I was not happy about it. To me, yes, it was a successful operation, but the mission was a failure. The supervisor lost the initiative when he chose to take the leader down in an open parking lot. He showed poor judgment and horrible execution due to ego. It had to be HIS plan and it had to be HIS idea.

Ego can kill officers. One famous police dashcam video shows a deputy, I believe, who was shot and killed by drug runners. In the video, you see the deputy wave off a back-up officer. The officer drives away. Shortly after, the deputy approaches a vehicle with two persons inside. He takes the driver out of the car and over to the rear of the vehicle. Shortly after that the passenger gets out of the car and a struggle ensues. Both of the bad guys shot and killed the deputy.

Ego gets officers in trouble too. When I have interacted with an individual and that individual had called me an asshole, I tend to agree with him or her. For one, it's a great way to quickly take away the individual's ability to escalate the situation. I've had people tell me "Fuck you." My response, to a male subject, was "Oh it's OK, I'm not gay." The individual quickly said, "I'm not gay." My response was "I didn't say you were gay, and what's wrong with being gay, there is nothing wrong with that." The person just walked away in a hurry. It's one of my funnier interactions.

How does an officer get in trouble? Someone calls the officer an asshole, the officer immediately arrests, and possibly assaults the individual. Not only did the officer make a bad arrest, because we do have Freedom of Speech in our constitution, but the officer let their ego take over and make a bad arrest. A lot of issues can be avoided if officers left their egos out of the job.

How many times have you or I been told, when we go into a gym, to leave our egos at the door? That's like an unwritten rule in lifting. Ego could seriously injure you when lifting weights that you are not ready for. So why can't we apply the same philosophy in policing? When officers train, it's nearly taboo to call an officer out for a mistake. They can't seem to swallow their pride and admit they made a mistake and learn from it.

I'd rather make a mistake in training than make a mistake out in the real world. SWAT teams are very good for calling out mistakes. If you zigged instead of zagged, you'd get called out. If your shooting has been hurting, you get called out. It is the nature of the beast. The rest of the law enforcement community needs to accept that and leave their egos at the door.

29

WHEN ONE OF US IS MURDERED

"Freedom does not come without a price. We may sometimes take for granted the many liberties we enjoy in America, but they have all been earned through the ultimate sacrifice paid by so many of the members of our armed forces."—Charlie Dent

It's so frequent these days. It's on the news nearly every day. An officer was shot and injured, an officer was assaulted, an officer was ambushed, an officer was shot and killed, an officer was stabbed and killed. President John F. Kennedy gave the law enforcement community a Memorial Day, May 14th. A day when we honor our brothers and sisters who died in the line of duty. Read President Kennedy's proclamation below:

April 10, 1962
By the President of the United States of America
A Proclamation

Whereas our law enforcement agencies play an essential role in safeguarding the rights and freedoms which have been guaranteed by the Constitution to every American citizen; and

Whereas it is important that people throughout our country know and understand the problems, duties, and responsibilities of their police departments and that members of our law enforcement agencies recognize their duty to serve the people by safeguarding life and property, by protecting them against violence or disorder, and by protecting the innocent against deception and the weak against oppression or intimidation; and

Whereas the Nation's police departments have grown to be modern and scientific law enforcement bodies which unceasingly provide a vital public service; and

Whereas the Congress, by a joint resolution approved June 21, 1961 (75 Stat. 94), has designated the week of May 13-19, 1962, as Police Week in recognition of the contribution the police officers of America have made to our civilization through their dedicated and selfless efforts in enforcing our laws and has also designated May 14th as Peace Officers Memorial Day in honor of the Federal, State, and municipal peace officers who have been killed or disabled in the line of duty; and

Whereas that resolution requests the President to issue a proclamation inviting the people of the United States to observe such period with appropriate ceremonies and activities:

Now, Therefore, I, John F. Kennedy, President of the United States of America, do hereby call upon the people of the United States, and upon all patriotic, civic, and educational organizations to observe the week of May 13-19,1962, as Police Week with appropriate ceremonies in which all of our people may join in commemorating police officers, past and present, who by their faithful and loyal devotion to their responsibilities have rendered a dedicated service to their communities and, in so doing, have established for themselves an enviable and enduring reputation for preserving the rights and security of all citizens.

I further call upon the people of the United States to observe Monday, May 14, 1962, as Peace Officers Memorial Day in honor of those peace officers who, through their courageous deeds, have lost their lives or have become disabled in the performance of duty.

In Witness Whereof, I have hereunto set my hand and caused the Seal of the United States of America to be affixed.

DONE at the City of Washington this tenth day of April in the year of our Lord nineteen hundred and sixty-two, and of the Independence of the United States of America, the one hundred and eighty-sixth.

JOHN F. KENNEDY
By the President:
DEAN RUSK,
Secretary of State
(John F. Kennedy, Proclamation 3466—Police Week and Peace Officers Memorial Day, 1962 Online by Gerhard Peters and John T. Woolley, The American Presidency Project)

National Law Enforcement Officers Memorial

Now that you've read this, I'm going to give a peek into the mind of a cop, when one of our brothers or sisters is killed in the line of duty.

I have been to several police funerals. Even one is one too many. The ones that really sting are those who were murdered. Murdered for doing their jobs, murdered because an evil person decided they didn't want to go to jail or face a judge. That officer was murdered because he or she went out to make someone accountable for their actions. This is what we do:

We gather in formation, several hundred officers, and even at times thousand, Honor Guard up front, uniformed officers behind them. Various law enforcement agencies gather for a day of mourning the loss of one of our murdered brothers or sisters. The murderer was apprehended, handcuffed, and sent away. We officers understand that we are not the jury nor the executioner, much as we want to act out whatever is going through our mind. We hold back. We honor the laws of the land. That's what is required of us.

When the murderer is apprehended, they get to go to jail. They aren't beaten to death, they aren't executed. The handcuffs are on them, so the fight is over. We officers are quiet, dazed and some have tearful eyes. A large procession of police officers follows the medical examiner's van because that is where the body of the slain officer is.

The murderer faces a judge the next day, gets breakfast, changes into a jail uniform, and is in court, in chains, and facing a judge. He or she is either assigned a lawyer or has already hired an attorney. Meanwhile, the family of the slain officer cries and screams while we officers provide support and comfort. The murderer is ordered held without bail and sent to the local jailhouse, held there until trial. The murderer gets prison clothing, food, and whatever else required. The family of the murdered officer is left with bills, pain, and that empty feeling that their whole world has crashed and burned.

We officers have not stopped working. We are still answering calls. We have to see a grief counselor. Some of us are still shaken but holding it together, while others can't go back to work yet. Those officer's shifts are then covered by other officers. We check on each other, we are silent, we go about our day. Area departments are asked to help the affected police department. Every officer in the area departments volunteers to assist. That way we can prepare for the funeral, and every officer of that department can be present. Area departments also cover that department's jurisdiction.

The day of the funeral the mood is somber; some officers joke around to ease the tension. We stand in formation. Bagpipes are played, prayers are made. The police department's Honor Guard folds the flag. The flag is then presented to the Chief of Police. The Chief walks over to the family of the murdered police officer, presents the flag and salutes the family.

NYPD funeral.
Photo source: Wikicommons

Then, the funeral is over. We return to work, business as usual. The affected department is also back. All officers are back to work, business as usual. There aren't any riots. No one is burning buildings, no looting. The officers are back protecting their respective communities.

Police week comes around. Thousands of police officers from all over the country go to Washington DC to honor their fallen. The names of officers recently murdered are etched on the memorial wall.

An officer tracing his colleague's name
Photo source: Wikicommons

Later that evening, we head to the National Mall, to call out the names of the officers that died that year. Each name is read, one at a time, and a bell is rung each time. We all hold candles in the air.

Then that ceremony, too, ends. The walk is eerily quiet. For thousands of us, our colleagues' memories linger. Soon after, the laughter begins, the sharing of stories, officers announce their retirements from the job. Officers from all over the country are there. They may not know each other, but in the end, they know that they are brothers and sisters. Black, White, Hispanic, Asian, Arab, it doesn't matter. We all bleed blue.

After a night of ceremonies, laughter, and story sharing, we return to our respective agencies. It's back to work and business as usual. We are out there capturing some really evil people. We are out there reminding you not to speed. We are out there helping an elderly woman walk across the street. We are holding the hands of a person we know is about to die. We are comforting victims of violence. We are tormented by a court system that sometimes frees bad people too quickly. We get frustrated when our voices aren't heard.

We are out there enforcing the laws that the people and politicians voted for. We are a reflection of society. We are the best in our society. We are the hunters of evil, and the last line of defense for the communities we swore to protect. When one of us is murdered we mourn, and we celebrate the officer who made the ultimate sacrifice.

Then it's back to business as usual.

30

FALSE REPORTING: A TRUE EPIDEMIC IN POLICING

"If you tell the truth, you don't have to remember anything." — Mark Twain

Most often, unless in a specialty unit, a patrol officer responds to a lot of calls for service (CFS). The CFS range from emergency 911 calls, to reports of larcenies and other crimes. The officer shows up, takes the report, or-- if the crime is ongoing -- the officer will either arrest or summons to court, depending on the level of the crime.

How many times have officers had to report to a CFS and discover that the situation was embellished, the reporting person lied, etc. I looked into it and researched a little and could not find any sort of solid data, percentages, etc. It isn't tracked. So, from my personal experience, I've had to deal with a lot of those types of calls that were embellished. With modern technology facilitating the use of anonymous tip apps, it's become even worse.

Early in my policing career, I answered a 911 call while working in the dispatch center of the headquarters of the police department. The caller reported that he was robbed at an ATM and gave me his location. I asked the typical who, what, where, when and what happened as police units were on their way. The caller said that a guy approached him and wanted to sell him some sugar in a bag.

The "victim" said he gave the unknown man money, and the guy took off. I remember laughing and said, "OH YOU MEAN, YOU DID A DRUG DEAL AND GOT RIPPED OFF." The man immediately became defensive and starting yelling profanities at me. The conversation did not last long after that. The "victim" hung up and we couldn't find him.

As technology advances, people are using apps on smartphones to report crimes, give anonymous tips, request police reports, etc. In my experience, a majority of these anonymous tips that come in are neighbor-on-neighbor disputes and complete bullshit. I've gone to calls where neighbors were arguing over a property line.

I have seen numerous anonymous tips come in and you can tell by the tone of the description that the reporting person hates a neighbor. So, they use the police to project their displeasure with the neighbor. It is disgusting half the time, or should I say most of the time.

Racism is a whole separate issue when it comes to reporting false crimes. I've seen it time and time again. The police get a CFS regarding a suspicious person. A description is put out by dispatch from the reporting party. We find the person, who is a person of color, and the poor person was there just walking through a park or going home, and someone tried to project their racism through the police. Most times, the individual the cops stop and question thinks he is being targeted by police, when in fact they were just responding to a CFS.

Now, here's a question I'm sure is burning in everyone's mind. Why don't we charge people for these false reports? Every state has laws regarding filing a false police report or misuse and abuse of 911. If we were to charge someone every time someone calls in a false report, the court system would be overloaded. Most of the time, if we do charge someone, they end up paying a small fine and that's as far as it goes. We would also end up charging people with mental illnesses who call police constantly for crimes that never occurred. Courts would dismiss those. That's the reality. We would need a separate court system solely dedicated to dealing with those types of charges.

I have only once charged someone for the misuse of 911 and filing a false police report. The person called the police claiming that someone destroyed his family's business. It turned out to be the person who called us. I charged him with malicious destruction of property, misuse of 911, and filing a false police report. Do you know how far it went in court? "Here is a slap on the wrist and don't do it again."

That's the reality of it.

How can this be fixed? Again, society needs to take a hard look at itself and ask, what's going on? From what I've seen, the opioid epidemic, mental health, the court system, police leaders, and elected officials all have a role in addressing this issue. They must work together to get to the root cause of it.

In this day of social media, Twitter, Facebook, Instagram, etc., police departments should continuously conduct public service announcements (PSA) to educate the public on the use and misuse of police services. Air the PSAs on local news outlets at least weekly. Educate the public about the punishments for false reports and charge people who lie to the police.

Police dispatch centers should have a list of individuals who are known to lie to police and effectively root out the cause of their constant calls to the police. Most of the time, it's a mental health issue and the police need to be able to work with medical professionals to get whatever services the person requires. Some of the solutions that have been tried, but not all police departments have the time, budget, or resources to address this issue.

In this present environment where everyone wants to blame the police for society's shortcomings, we'd probably have a better chance to ruck march barefoot on glass than see all the entities I described actually work together.

QUIET INTENSITY

Briefing done
Operation is a go.
Put on my kit.
Radio check
Light check
Weapons check
I load a magazine, bolt released, bullet in the chamber.
A sound all too familiar
For those who answer the call.
I enter the bearcat
With the rest of the team,
Engine roars,
The beast comes to life,
The loud hum of the bearcat
Inside the belly of the beast.
I sit, quiet, reserved,
I look around, the same look on us all,
A quiet intensity,
A quiet resolve,
Voice in the intercom, "one minute out,"
I take three deep breaths.
Doors open.
I step into the arena.

31

EFFECTS-BASED OPERATIONS IN LAW ENFORCEMENT

"Be extremely subtle even to the point of formlessness. Be extremely mysterious even to the point of soundlessness. Thereby you can be the director of the opponent's fate."— Sun Tzu

I was sitting in a parking lot recently with one of my colleagues. My unit was conducting a surveillance operation of a couple of bad guys in the area. We were on a little break. As we were talking, we saw Oregon had passed a decriminalization bill on all drugs including drugs like Heroin and Cocaine. We were both astonished and concerned about what life in Oregon is going to look like for its citizens.

From what I've read, the people of Oregon voted for this new law. My question is, why was it even on the ballot? Then a great point was made by my colleagues: "You know, the Army has some of the best training when it comes to first, second, third order effects. These politicians need some lessons about that." What he was referring to were Effects-Based Operations. I paused for a second and he was 100% correct.

I was part of a unit, in the city I work in, that worked with various outreach groups and programs in an attempt to help those suffering from addiction. A majority of the addicts I dealt with were not addicts by choice. An addict by choice is a person who decided to try a drug then got hooked on it. The addicts I dealt with were the product of the opioid epidemic that was caused by Big Pharma and doctors who over-prescribed pain relievers for their patients. Most of these addicts had either been severely injured in a car accident or were injured playing a sport.

The thing is though, they were so caught up with their addiction, they would relapse. We wouldn't arrest the addict because that does not solve anything. We would help them find beds at rehab centers, guide them as they got sober, and even go after the drug dealers who would entice them to relapse. We went through a lot of issues because our government did not see the long-term effects, and big Pharma, other than making a boatload of money, did not anticipate the long-term effects.

In the Army, we learned the following when planning an operation: What is the overall objective? What is the commander's intent? What is the order of effects? Let's apply this philosophy to policing.

What are Effects-Based Operations?

The military defines Effects-Based Operations (EBO) as operations conceived and planned in a systems framework that considers the full range of direct, indirect, and cascading effects as those effects that may, with different degrees of probability, be achieved by the application of military, diplomatic, psychological, and economic instruments. Now, this seems very complex and it involves a multi-discipline/unit approach to achieve an objective.

How can this apply to law enforcement?

Narcotics units, gang units, SWAT, and various other units could also do their jobs in going after the major players in the narcotics world. To me, those are your hammer units or, in military terms, your Direct-Action (DA) units, which also include Patrol Division. But what about unconventional units like Problem-Oriented Policing, Community Service, and a whole list of units that use unconventional methods to go after the root cause of an issue? Not everything we do requires a DA approach. As police, we must embrace unconventional methods.

I'll present to you an example of how an investigation begins and ends. A complaint comes in, such as "there is drug dealing at 123 Main St". A narcotic unit sets up an investigation which leads to a search warrant and the eventual arrest of suspect(s). The next phase is now in the court. For us, as cops, once the case is in court, we pretty much are done and move on to the next case because we don't control what happens in court, contrary to popular belief and shows like CSI.

An EBO approach to this problem would be a coordinated effort from all the units at the police department. The narcotics unit, patrol division, and other DA units conduct their investigations, arrests, car stops, and all sorts of other DA-type activities. After all this is done, or even during, the unconventional police units are in there, fixing whatever issues that might be causing these drug dealers to move into these neighborhoods. Whether it is bad lighting, or broken window theory, unconventional units would take ownership of these issues and start to work on them.

Different Types of EBOs

An example is what my unconventional unit did on a problem location. There was a house in the city I work in. We had constant complaints of parties, drugs, and all sorts of other disruptions. The occupants of the house were not too welcoming of police or neighbors telling them to quiet down.

My unit took ownership of this problem. We decided to start working with the neighborhood and the occupants of that house. First, we addressed a problem with overgrown trees on the lot. The tree branches were hanging over the power lines that fed directly to the house. We assisted the occupants to arrange for the electric company to come and cut down those branches so the occupants would not lose electricity in bad weather. When a suspected drug deal occurred, the unit went after and stopped the individuals, regardless of whether an arrest was made or not. It put the word out. This house and its occupants were "on the radar." After a short while, they moved on to another city.

Here is another EBO that my unit coordinated. There was a problem house in the city to which the police department had to respond numerous times a day. It was taxing on our ability to take care of the rest of the city. The typical calls for service at this location were fights, assaults, assaults with a dangerous weapon, stabbings, drug dealing, and domestic abuse. The homeowners used their home as a rooming house. They did not care about the issues; they only cared about the rent money, which was about $500 per room, and/or the occupants' EBT cards (Food Stamps).

My unit analyzed all the issues with that house. One day, there was another stabbing at the residence. Multiple police and fire units showed up. I walked into the house and made several observations of health and building code violations. After everything was settled and arrests were made, I called various city departments and started the process to get the city to go to the home and condemn it. The next day, all the various city departments went to the residence and were horrified at the living conditions at the house. They immediately condemned the house.

Unconventional Policing Unit

Word got out very quickly to all the landlords in the city that had these rooming houses. They printed out the article from the local paper and would use it as an example to their residents. They were afraid of being the next condemned home. The overall effect of EBO worked. The word spread like wildfire. The results? Slumlords were put on notice. These problem houses disappeared.

The utilization of crime analysis, direct action units, and unconventional units in a police department make it perfect to use EBO in certain situations. Police departments and their personnel need to approach certain problems in their respective communities in a multi-discipline approach. It takes coordination and all the units working together to achieve the goal. The days of each department unit working separately must change.

I have seen it time and time again where the patrol division steps on the toes of the narcotics division. Even specialized units in the departments do not talk to each other and end up overlapping the same targets and cases. EBO can take away those overlapping problems and units will have to work together. You can see where I am going with this. Policing requires a level of teamwork. Unfortunately, at times, some cops want to be heroes and work on their own. That's when issues arise, and cases start to fall apart. Let's make that change and approach policing as a team.

Let's go back to Oregon and this new drug law that was passed. Did the state think this through? Did they think of the long-term effects? How about the influx of addicts coming to the state? Did they think about drug dealers utilizing these laws to their advantage? Are the rehab facilities already set up? What are the first, second, and third order effects? Are social services prepared to deal with addicts? My experience tells me no.

Where I work, when possession of marijuana was decriminalized and became a misdemeanor subject to a fine. The courts were not ready to hear any of the appeals. What happened? Police stopped issuing tickets. Why issue tickets when there isn't any due process associated with them? These hard drugs that Oregon recently decriminalized are extremely destructive. I understand why they decriminalized some drugs but why didn't the law require that, when an addict is arrested, the court immediately must send the addict to a rehab facility? I think that would be more logical. Punishment could become something like community service instead of jail time. Did they have an EBO in place and coordinate with law enforcement?

Politicians, lawyers, police, and other professions would benefit from training in EBO. As Marcus Aurelius stated, "what we do now, echoes in eternity." Every little action we do has a ripple effect. I think most people have lost sight of the endgame and get fixated on putting a band-aid on a problem. Let's get to the root cause of any problem and make a permanent fix. That's a way to truly care for and serve this great nation of ours.

32

THERE IS A DIFFERENCE BETWEEN BEHAVIORAL PROFILING AND RACIAL PROFILING

"People will do anything, no matter how absurd, in order to avoid facing their own souls. One does not become enlightened by imagining figures of light, but by making the darkness conscious."— *Carl Jung*

I took a college course some years back. At that point, I'd been a police officer for about three years. The course centered around the issues of racial profiling, including the history of racial profiling. The definition of racial profiling, according to dictionary.com, is: "the use of race or ethnicity as grounds for suspecting someone of having committed an offense." This article isn't about statistics or numbers. This article is deeper than that.

In addition to racial profiling, I am also going to address a method of police training that has been going on for as long as I can remember: training law enforcement officers to analyze behavior. Before diving into this subject, it is important to cover some terminology and definitions. On a side note, I love it when suspects use this language. These types are called "jailhouse lawyers." It makes my job so much more fun. Keep in mind, these definitions vary from state to state.

Let's go over some terminology so you can follow along (keep in mind, they vary state to state but are very similar):

- Hunch: An intuition or "gut feeling" about something. An officer's instincts. This allows the officer to approach and talk to a person. The person doesn't have to talk to the cop. [Author's Note: that does not mean if the cop wants to have a nice conversation to make their time go by, you automatically assume you are being targeted. A lot of times, we just talk to people. That's our nature.]
- Reasonable Suspicion: This is more than a hunch and it involves specific facts that lead an objective police officer to suspect a crime has occurred or will occur.
- Probable Cause: This means, more likely than not, that the suspect has committed or is committing a crime, or evidence will be found in a particular place.

There are many more terms I had to learn in the academy, but those three are important for this discussion. For example, a police officer is patrolling a neighborhood and observes a subject pacing back and forth at a local park. The officer then observes the subject walk toward a car and conduct a hand-to-hand drug transaction. This goes beyond a hunch and straight to reasonable suspicion right away. This elevates the officer's ability to stop and detain the two individuals and even to arrest if need be. This is a perfect world scenario that an officer is able to investigate every once in a while.

Notice, I did not add race to this scenario. This was based strictly on behavior. This was behavior profiling and it takes years to develop. I have close to 20 years on this job and am still developing mine. Police cadets or student officers get some exposure in the classroom, but this type of training takes a great deal of time. It is up to individual departments to invest in their officers and send them to quality training.

I'm going to backtrack a little to my racial profiling class. The professor gave me this particular scenario as he knew I was a police officer: A Hispanic male robbed a store and fled. He was wearing a white shirt and blue jeans. He asked me what I would do. I responded by stating that I would look for a Hispanic male wearing a white shirt and blue jeans. The professor responded, "that's racial profiling." I disagreed and said that if I got a call from dispatch telling me who to look for, that's who I'd look for. If the store clerk provided me a description of the robber, I was going to look for someone that looked like that. I have stopped people that were wearing the same outfits as described by victims and other officers. If they turned out not to be the one officers were looking for or if the store owner told me that person was not the suspect, I would let him go on his way with a Coke and a smile.

Here is one example of racial profiling: Dispatch received a report, and the caller described a suspicious person walking outside of a strip mall. The dispatcher asked the caller, "OK, what makes him suspicious?" The caller states, "well he's black." Another example: I received a call from dispatch of what was described as a black male wearing a black t-shirt and blue jeans who was harassing people. So, I made my way to the location and saw someone fitting that profile. Prior to engaging him, I observed him. He was just sitting in the park. I approached him and we had a nice conversation. He was taking a leisurely walk. I left him alone and went about my day. These are two examples of racial profiling that were not officer initiated, but rather were profiled by the persons who called 911. I'd be rich if I had a dollar for every bogus call that comes in. But the blame is always directed at the police officer. In reality, a lot of these issues stem from people calling the police because of their own biases and prejudices.

I want you to ask yourself, is the problem really "all" officers? Is it a combination of factors? I've dealt with racist store clerks, racist firemen, and countless others. The difference is that in law enforcement we are entrusted with a huge responsibility of enforcing the laws of that particular state. The saying, *"Justice is blind"* holds true for a lot of officers. I'd say the majority. *The minuscule percent that does not believe that justice is blind is the problem with law enforcement.* They are still human, brought up a certain way, with different experiences. I'm not excusing them; I am merely pointing out that the profession still has the human element. I only hope that the bad cops get weeded out early in a background investigation or early on in their career before they tarnish the badge and what we, the vast majority, stand for.

33

A CAPABLE COP IS A CONFIDENT COP: QUALITY VS. PROFICIENCY

"It is the power of the mind to be unconquerable."— Seneca

I have a question for the civilian reader population. How often do you think police train on tactics, firearms, first aid, CPR, and use of force? Once a year, twice a year? You will be surprised by how often police officers train in this profession. Most of the time, it's a check-the-box type of training just to say a cop is "qualified" in firearms, tactics, etc. To me, qualifying and proficiency are two very separate things. I think most will agree with that statement. I'm going to give you, the reader, a glimpse into the training of law enforcement officers, mostly around this concept of qualifying.

Some police departments invest in their officers, while most do not. Most state and local budgets do not allocate enough money for police training. I've seen both ends of the spectrum. For the most part, though, most police departments ensure their officers are *qualified* -- but are they *proficient?*

In the Army, when one attends basic training, you are handed a soldier's handbook as part of your in-processing. That handbook details all the core tasks in which soldiers must be proficient—everything from weapons maintenance to tactics. The Army lays it all out for every private, outlining what he or she is expected to be trained in.

Policing is not the same. Sure, there are core tasks you're expected to qualify in, but there isn't a proficiency standard. Nor is there enough training available to ensure each officer is proficient in their core tasks.

What are the core tasks for police officers? Firearms, Defensive Driving, CQB (close quarters combat), defensive tactics, less-than-lethal weapons, constitutional law, criminal law (your jurisdiction), use of force, code of conduct, radio communication, counter-ambush techniques, felony motor vehicle takedown, introductory psychology, basic negotiation, behavioral profiling, traffic stops, proper handcuffing methods and physical fitness.

What I described to you is a basic recruit academy. Academies range from 6 weeks to 6 months, depending on which part of the United States you're from. After the academy, again, depending on which part of the U.S. you're from, you may not train again. If you train, it'll be a yearly or bi-annual weapons qualification and a yearly in-service. In-service is typically a week-long course to re-certify or qualify officers in some of the core tasks.

All that is required of police departments is that their officers qualify, not demonstrate proficiency in any of the core tasks. I'm a firearms instructor; I can't tell you how often my blood pressure increases when some of the officers coming up to the firing line can barely hit the target. A study in the journal Force Science explains:

"Researchers analyzed 149 real-life OISs (officer-involved shootings) recorded over 15 years by Dallas (TX) PD. In nearly half of these encounters, officers firing at a single suspect delivered "complete inaccuracy." That is, they missed the target entirely.

In 15 incidents, the total number of rounds fired could not be determined. But in the 134 cases where researchers could establish that figure, they calculated the "incredible" hit rate at merely 35%. In other words, more than six out of ten rounds fired were misses.

"Unfortunately," the study says, "the data do not provide a clear picture of what happened with these [errant] rounds, but, at worst, they struck other officers or innocent bystanders."

The research team, Dr. Christopher Donner and Nicole Popovich of the Criminal Justice department at Loyola University in Chicago, note that "although the amount—and quality—of firearms training received by officers over the last century has increased considerably, there appears to have been little improvement in shooting accuracy."

What this means to me is police officers are not proficient in their use of firearms. Proficiency is very different from qualifying. I'll go over the firearms qualification that officers must accomplish yearly. Keep in mind that what I'm going to discuss is a standard firearms qualification. Some police departments train their officers a lot more than others.

Depending on the size of the police department and state requirements, typical firearms qualifications are 50 rounds. Distance varies from 3 yards to 15 yards. Officers also shoot at a stationary target. This qualifies officers; that's it. This does not test proficiency. Most cops only do the yearly minimum and that's it. Only a small percentage of them will go shoot at a range to work on the fundamentals and become proficient.

Proficiency is measured through real firearms training. It tests every officer's physical, psychological, and physiological state. We should treat firearms training like it should be, actual firearms training.

Officers should be required to be proficient in taking apart, cleaning, putting together, and firing their weapons. They need to have a working knowledge of the weapons assigned to them and the caliber of ammunition they carry.

Let's switch gears. The public sees all kinds of different police vehicles. During the police academy, I was trained to drive a Ford Crown Victoria. It was a one-week Emergency Vehicle Operation Course

(EVOC). The goal of the course was for the officer to learn how the police car handles and what it can do and can't do. I have not accomplished any sort of EVOC training since the academy. I've been issued other cruisers over the years. Driving a car down the road is a lot different from driving with lights and sirens responding to a gunshot call. I believe EVOC is a core task that officers need to be tested on annually or bi-annually. Again, the officer will get more proficient when driving with blue lights and sirens. Officers will be more proficient during high-speed pursuits.

In the end, there are core tasks that officers must be proficient in. Qualifying is not enough. Qualifying is a CYA for police departments just to show that an officer can shoot a target. The real test is proficiency and with proficiency comes confidence.

A confident cop is a capable cop.

34

WHY APPLYING SPECIAL FORCES DOCTRINE IS ESSENTIAL TO LAW ENFORCEMENT

U.S. Army Special Forces and Law Enforcement? NO!!! THAT'S MILITARIZATION OF POLICE! But is it? Let's discuss this. What do I mean by this, what can a police department use from U.S. Army Special Forces? Training? Leadership? Close Quarter Battle? Or am I referring to something more? Let me be clear, in no way am I saying that police officers are Special Forces. The reason I am drawing this analogy is to get you, the reader, to think about it.

These days we are inundated with news about U.S. Army Special Forces conducting raids or engaging in firefights throughout the world. Movies and TV shows imply Special Forces members, like Rambo, take on entire battalions of combat soldiers. Totally unrealistic. Likewise, for police, TV shows and movies have always idolized the renegade cop who doesn't care about the rules, uses extremely excessive force, but gets the job done. Again, totally unrealistic.

Now let's look at the structure of a police department. Although each police department in the country is different based on the needs of their community, I'm going to paint a general picture. A police department has a Chief/Sheriff/Superintendent, Deputy Chief(s), Major(s), Captain(s), Lieutenants(s), Sergeant(s), and Patrol Officers. This is the basic chain of command for any police department.

Now let's examine the various units within a police department: Patrol Division, Gang Units, K9 Units, SWAT, Street Crimes Unit, Problem-Oriented Policing Unit, Community Service Unit, Bomb Technicians, Narcotic Unit, Anti-Crime Unit, Community Service Unit, an Airwing Unit, a Maritime Unit, Major Crimes Unit (Detectives), and an Intelligence Unit. I may have missed one or two more but again this is a general description of how major police departments are structured. Smaller departments commonly pool resources and request mutual aid from larger departments. I am going to break them down further and draw the analogy of how Special Forces Doctrine applies to Law Enforcement.

There are many missions of the Special Forces, but I am going to focus on two of their missions: Unconventional Warfare (UW) and Direct Action (DA) missions. Patrol Officers, SWAT, K9 Units, Narcotic Unit, and Street Crimes Units are your DA units. Their primary mission is to be that brute force for the police department--the hammer. Narcotics, Street Crimes, K9, and various other similar units investigate, exploit, cultivate, and target specific individuals within the community that are involved in drugs, guns, shootings, killings, and other very violent offenses.

Problem-Oriented Policing Units, Community Service Units, Intelligence Units, and other similar units are the UW units of the police department. Their primary mission is what we call "quality of life" type of issues in their respective cities. What are quality of life issues? The broken window theory is an example. The broken window theory was proposed by James Wilson and George Kelling in 1982. They used the phrase "broken window" as a metaphor for disorder within neighborhoods. Their theory links disorder and incivility within a community.

Let's define UW. The Department of Defense (DOD) defines UW as activities to enable a resistance movement or insurgency to coerce, disrupt or overthrow a government or occupying power through and with an underground, auxiliary, and guerrilla force in a denied area.

How is this applied in law enforcement? Let's say for example a known drug dealer is plaguing the area with Fentanyl. A police UW unit would go into the affected area, work with the neighborhood, talk to the addicts, teach people in the neighborhood how to detect drug dealings. Eventually, the dealer or dealers could be arrested.

The people of that neighborhood would feel more empowered and prepared to deal with any future issue and the trust in the police would improve. This is winning hearts and minds. Take the part of UW's definition of overthrowing an occupying power, i.e., drug dealer, and add enabling a resistance movement, i.e., a neighborhood, to assist in overthrowing (arresting) the occupying power (drug dealer). How do we win hearts and minds? By embedding ourselves in the community-- not sitting in a cruiser with the windows up and not talking to people. Law enforcement wins hearts and minds by playing sports with the neighborhood youth, striking up a conversation with people in a park, checking in on businesses, or helping an older person cross the street. This is how to earn their trust and respect. Special Forces have been doing this for decades. They go into hostile villages and work to get the entire village on their side through UW.

Police UW units could apply this theory by going to the heart of issues in a neighborhood. They should not just focus on criminals, but they should ask the question "why." They make partners of people from within the community. They dress in regular clothes, drive regular cars instead of police cars, and are very personable officers who can truly make an impact in a neighborhood. They solve problems through UW.

Now let's change the term "Unconventional Warfare" to policing terms. Let's call it Unconventional Policing (UP). What does that mean? UP means not every situation requires handcuffs. It is looking at a problem and solving it by thinking "outside the box." This is effective because it employs unconventional methods to teach the community to help itself.

A UP unit I had the pleasure of being a part of was called the Problem-Oriented Policing Unit in the city where I work. It was a brand-new unit and two officers and a lieutenant (LT) were selected as members. Another officer and I, under the command of the LT, met to discuss our mission and purpose. They were broad and left a lot of room for imagination to execute. We were given a long leash; we didn't respond to calls for service. Instead, our mission was to find the root causes of issues in our city and fix them. We had to deal with addicts, parolees, violent offenders, persons who cause the most calls for service, locations that cause the most calls for service, etc.

EPILOGUE

I have been many things in my life: a son, an immigrant, a soldier, a husband, a father, a police officer, a small business owner, and now, an author. And I am deeply proud of each and every one of them. It has been my great pleasure to write, and share, the stories you read in the previous pages. If you are, were, or want to be a member of the military or a first responder, I hope that this book will be of use to you, either now or in the future.

I have no way of knowing what the future holds, but I do know that we will need men and women of courage, candor, and commitment to uphold our values and protect our way of life. A life of service to others is not easy, and is full of dangers. But you can do it if you set yourself on The Resolute Path.

ABOUT THE AUTHOR

Ayman Kafel: Father, Husband, Soldier, Police Officer, and Author

Ayman Kafel survived two civil wars in Africa and Lebanon before immigrating to the United States in 1988. After witnessing the horrors of September 11, 2001, Ayman enlisted in the Army National Guard and deployed to Iraq in 2005. While there, he conducted over 30,000 miles of combat patrols and missions, and coordinated and worked with various units in the Army due to his ability to speak Arabic.

After he returned from war, Ayman decided to continue serving his country and community by becoming a police officer, a profession he has served in for over 15 years. He first started his career at the MBTA Police Department in 2007. After three years as a transit cop, Ayman transferred to the Attleboro Police Department in 2011. While in Attleboro, he went from uniformed patrol to the newly formed Problem-Oriented Policing (POP) Unit in 2012. The POP team's main objectives are to reduce the calls for service at the top ten locations, conduct directed problem-solving of issues designated by the Chief of Police, perform opiate addiction intervention and recovery efforts, and oversee incarcerated prisoner re-entry intervention visits.

In 2013 Ayman tried out and was selected for the Metropolitan Law Enforcement Council SWAT team. As a Metro SWAT Operator, his duties included resolving high-risk tactical / hostage situations, high-risk warrant service operations, search and rescue operations, tactical waterborne operations, covert and undercover tactical operations, exceptional circumstances such as crowd control, rural searches, terrorism response, and counter-terror deployment, special dignitary protection/escort/perimeter protection.

In 2016, he was selected to become a detective at the police department. As a detective, Ayman conducted complex investigations of major crimes, including homicides in the city of Attleboro. He also gained experience in writing, swearing in, and issuing search and arrest warrants from district courts and superior courts, and he testified in Grand Jury and criminal trials. Shortly after that, he was selected to become a DEA Task Force Officer (TFO) and also tried out and successfully passed the DEA Special Response Unit Certification Course. As a DEA TFO, Ayman conducted numerous complex drug investigations, including writing and swearing in on multiple federal search and arrest warrants. He testified in the federal grand jury and criminal trials.

As a DEA Special Response Team Operator, he was selected as an assistant team leader. In this role, he assisted in tactics and firearms training and the planning and execution of operations all over New England. He also assisted in the development and creation of new standard operating procedures for the team. After 6 years assigned to the DEA, he returned back to the Attleboro Police Department and took command of the Problem-Oriented Policing Unit.

While in command of the POP, Ayman led a team of investigators focused on problem-oriented policing and partnered with public and private sector agencies to overcome challenges in the neighborhoods served. He also coordinated with the Community Council of Bristol County (CCBC). He initiated a ride- along program for a social worker and a recovery coach to address mental health issues and overdoses affecting the city of Attleboro. In November of 2022, he was promoted to the rank of Sergeant and is assigned to the patrol division as a Road Sergeant.

Ayman is not only an active police officer but also a law enforcement instructor and has taught across the East Coast of the United States. He offers a wide variety of training, such as advanced patrol tactics, mechanical breaching courses, designated marksman, and Human Performance under duress. He is the founder and owner of Hybrid Wolf Blue Line Strategies, LLC. A veteran-owned training and consulting company for Law Enforcement officers and agencies. He combines his military and law enforcement experience to bring much-needed cutting-edge training to the law enforcement profession.

www.ingramcontent.com/pod-product-compliance
Lightning Source LLC
Chambersburg PA
CBHW040854120626
46551CB00001B/15